Practical advice for emerging authors.

The Diction Dude Essential Guide to Getting Started as a Professional Writer

Jason E. Gillikin

August 12, 2020

Lakeshore Technical

Colophon

Ebook ISBN: 978-0-9863806-5-5
Print ISBN: 978-0-9863806-6-2
Library of Congress Control Number (print): 2020935511

Version History

Version 1.0 published in August 2020 by Lakeshore Technical. Printed in the United States of America. Distributed by Lakeshore Literary and Ingram.

Hone your craft. Find your voice. Join your tribe.

—The Diction Dude

Contents

List of Figures

List of Tables

Preliminaries

Why It's So Damned Hard | 1

For most people, banging out a manuscript in Microsoft Word and then shipping it off to a high-powered New York agent isn't the typical pathway to literary success. Rather, aspiring wordsmiths often stumble in the dark, trying to make sense of a nonsensical industry, until they meet with failure more than 99.99 percent of the time. Yet the frustration they feel about their early writing experiences isn't exactly unwarranted; the publishing industry is notorious for not preparing emerging authors for the discipline it takes to become a commercially successful author of long-form fiction.

1.1 Wandering Aimlessly

THE BIGGEST CHALLENGE facing emerging writers sources from bad advice about getting started. People eager to become famous authors approach the table, in almost every circumstance, with a limited understanding of the industry and with substantial blind spots about their comparative readiness and skill level. These knowledge gaps—many of which aren't even their fault—condemn almost all of them to a journey more difficult that it needs to be. Those few who wind their way to the finish line sometimes advance on their merits, but more often, they thrive merely because they were lucky or connected (or both) at a critical pivot point early in their literary career.

As a small-press leader, I frequently encountered these knowledge gaps in my interactions with aspiring writers. It took me a while to contextualize what I saw. For a while, at first, I'd review an obviously off-base query package and wonder, "Why on earth does this writer think that this stuff is worth querying?" It wasn't until I spent more time talking to emerging writers at conferences and literary events that I started to understand that the problem wasn't with them, *per se*—rather, it arose from a lack of solid information to help new industry entrants to find their way, even when they overachieved in their attempt to arm themselves with useful knowledge.

I'm not fond of blaming vast, impersonal systems for the challenges that individual people face. Yet I eventually concluded that even good-faith efforts to learn collided with an industry that, in some ways, reaps the benefit of a poorly informed supplier base. Wandering aimlessly hurts writers, but this confusion empowers a not-small-enough cluster of bad actors working in the shadowy margins of the publishing ecosystem.

Seven industry-specific incentive misalignments, plus an additional two author-specific blind spots, bedevil aspiring writers. It's worth starting this book with an extended discussion of these nine structural headwinds because each should sketch a "here be dragons" segment upon the mental map by which you chart your course to success. They highlight why it's so hard for emerging writers to get a toehold as commercially published authors—but, conversely, avoiding those dragons improves your odds of landing your first contract.

Incentive Mismatches

Far from operating as a well-oiled machine, the publishing industry is beset by a large number of stakeholders with competing—and sometimes contradictory—objectives. Let's explore seven of these mismatches.

The industry doesn't help new writers because insiders lack incentive to spread vital business acumen. Many corporate jobs across most industries require a bachelor's degree even if the work could be successfully completed by a high-school diplomate. Because a small-enough proportion of the workforce possesses a college degree, this requirement sharply limits the number of applications for any given white-collar job. Resumes may be dismissed out-of-hand, and objectively, based on the presence or absence of a required-on-paper credential. First you get through the formal box-checking, then you get to substantive review by a recruiter, then you become a finalist and actually compete on your merits with the hiring manager. It's just not possible for hiring managers to surrender those intermediary triage points and grant interviews to every applicant for every job. They need a filter.

Publishing, however, lacks an objective competency filter—at least for authors. In publishing, there's no requirement that querying writers and poets earn a bachelor's in English or a Master of Fine Arts. In fact, in most cases, editors and agents place effectively no *formal* screens whatsoever on author qualifications—apart, perhaps, from possessing a valid U.S. taxpayer identification number. Although most literary agents examine a person's publication history, academic background, and life story as part of the query-evaluation process, the industry rarely stipulates mandatory and objective criteria for automagically screening the number of "applicants" for a given book slot.

And the number-of-applicants problem is huge. Hundreds or even thousands of authors compete for a single book contract or prestigious journal acceptance. There's simply no way to implement an industry-wide multi-stage triage, using black-or-white criteria, for something as creatively complex as writing. So what to do?

Unlike in other industries where what matters is the credential and not necessarily the formatting of your resume, in publishing what matters is the overall effectiveness of your query package as an inducement to deeply engage with the substance of your pitch. That query package (or, for non-fiction, your book proposal) marks the first and likely only point of contact between the author and the gatekeepers of the industry who extend contracts and license agreements. If you fail the query process, you fail as a commercially viable author, because almost no overworked gatekeeper looks past a "bad" query hoping a good manuscript lies beneath.

Most query packages are utterly abysmal. Almost every editor or agent who screens unsolicited manuscripts will attest that well north of 75 percent of all queries get rejected in fewer than 10 seconds. That's all it takes to see that the person *or* the pitched book aren't viable for the targeted market. And probably another 20 percent get rejected within two minutes. It's five percent or less that actually incur any substantive engagement, and of those, only a tiny sliver earn an acceptance letter.

There's no vast industry conspiracy to make "effective querying" some sort of classified bit of data that you only access through a special training course or membership in a secret society. Because, as individual editors and agents, *we want to see good stuff*. We really do. We want beautiful stories to grace books with our logos proudly affixed to the spines. We want everyone to earn a fat, happy paycheck. Likewise, there's no "one weird trick" to querying or a paint-by-numbers template that differentiates successful from unsuccessful queries—no shortcut to the top of the slush pile.

The only way to develop an effective query package is to understand your industry and to be clear-eyed about your strengths and weaknesses as an author. Those bits of knowledge not only inform the query package, but also *the substance of the work you pitch*.

But because queries serve as the sieve between the world and editorial decision-makers, the publishing industry maintains a vested interest in not teaching authors how to manipulate its gatekeeping system—i.e., no one's especially eager to offer useful advice about getting a second look when the underlying content isn't ready for prime time, because "good" queries for "bad" stories consume precious review time.[1]

1: In scientific terms: Great queries for mediocre books constitute a Type I (false positive) error; bad queries for good books yield a Type II (false negative) error. Editorial systems are designed to minimize Type I error at the expense of Type II error, because this approach generates the least amount of wasted time, even if occasionally good but poorly pitched manuscripts never obtain a fair read.

Turnover and burnout is so high that individual insiders lack the fire in the belly to engage in independent outreach to authors. The sad truth about the publishing industry is that people who work hard to get those coveted New York acquisitions-editor jobs get paid less than a living wage, in Manhattan, to work sometimes 60 or more hours per week.[1] They spend just a few years in the role before burning out, working on average 18 to 36 months then "retiring" to less-stressful book-marketing jobs. Relatively few editors still laboring in the trenches of Big Publishing enjoy meaningful seniority—top management, maybe, but the base of the pyramid is distressingly transient.

The people who have the knowledge lack the time; when they finally get the time, they prefer to do anything other than reopen the wounds of their prior agony.

The sometimes adversarial nature of author-publisher relationships prompts most publishers to remain silent to avoid social-media ire. A small but outspoken cadre of bloggers and tweeters view the author-publisher relationship as a zero-sum game. That is, they view any action that potentially helps publishers as *intrinsically* writer-harmful.[2] This approach isn't helpful and it isn't accurate.

More to the point, the community of some authors who've deputized themselves as the publishing police reduces the incentive for publishers to offer useful advice about how to succeed. Why should industry pros bother? Much of their how-to advice is dismissed with a cynical eye by less-than-successful authors who dwell atop the food chain of by-author-for-author websites. Some of those sites offer phenomenal value to aspiring authors; the website for the Science Fiction Writers of America, for example, delivers superb resources for writers. Other sites, however, wallow in mediocre toxicity—including some well-known submission-tracking sites that presume to rate publishers against author-reported metrics. The voices that could help people separate wheat from chaff about the industry's inner workings prefer to err on the side of silence, because debating the ill-informed zealots brings nothing but grief.

Thus, the most critical voice at the table—*the people who actually understand how the industry works*—silences itself because it's easier to disengage than to speak up. Emerging authors are not served well by this dynamic.

Many former mid-list writers pivoted away from genre fiction and toward writing advice as mid-list revenues dwindle, but because these self-appointed experts lack meaningful experience as publishers or agents, their advice is sometimes more harmful than helpful. Years ago, a mid-list author—that is, an author who generated one or more reasonably competent yet eminently forgettable genre-fiction books each year—wrote novels. But mid-list writing has effectively dried up over the mid-to-late 2010s.[3] Some of those writers, eager to maintain a revenue stream, repositioned themselves as expert author coaches. They draft books about becoming successful writers, they host podcasts, they pen guest posts on each other's how-to-be-an-author blogs—and for the most part, they're leading emerging writers astray.

One commonality of this new "I'm a successful author so I can teach you how to be one, too" subgenre is that much of its work product presents a skewed understanding of how publishers price and mitigate risk. These authors frequently fail to acknowledge the degree to which their own dumb luck or back-channel connections got them on the mid-list in the first place, so they confuse the accidents of their success with readily transferrable rules for others' success. Similarly, because most of them have never worked as publishers or agents, they lack critical insight into the very real problem of stakeholder misalignment, particularly as it relates to marketing and distribution. The phenomenon is akin to the person who, having just knit a few woolen mittens that sold well enough at the county craft fair, decides that she's now an expert on sheep shearing and yarn making and the effective administration of fabric stores.

You cannot thrive as a traditionally published author of repute if you lack a solid mental map of the various stakeholder roles—agents, publishers, editors, authors, distributors, commercial buyers, libraries, retailers, reviewers, graphic designers, printers, freelance artists, etc.—and how those roles pursue sometimes contradictory economic outcomes. Publishing as a business isn't about creative writing or great storytelling or literary art. It's about *generating profit for the publisher, because the publisher assumes all of the financial risk of the book's potential failure*. If you cannot navigate this fraught web of stakeholders, each of which operates with imperfect knowledge and cross-purposed incentives, then your success correspondingly declines.

It's probably the case that these former mid-listers really do enjoy some degree of industry-wide knowledge, but a deep review of the literature in preparation for this book suggests that almost none of them effectively translate the business side of the equation into print. Overwhelmingly, books by this class of writer offer a lot of upbeat, fluffy writing advice and cheerful exhortations to keep on keepin' on. But valuable perspectives from the editors' desk? Not so much.

Few academic programs offer substantial instruction about the business of writing. I once ran a regionally focused micro press that, each semester, hosted several interns for academic credit. As we surveyed baccalaureate-level writing programs, we discovered that no institution of higher education that we surveyed—and we checked with a dozen in the Upper Midwest—offered, even as an elective, a course to Creative Writing students about the publishing industry or about the business of writing. These programs churned out people who knew how to be *writers*, but not people who knew how to be *published authors*. There's a huge difference between these terms. Most people can, with guidance, become proficient writers. Most people can, with guidance, become comfortable with the industry. But the overlap of "writers" with "people who understand the industry" remains depressingly small. Higher-ed institutions, more than any other stakeholder, ought to prepare their graduates for a life in publishing. It's not clear that many do.

Part of the challenge relates to the logic model of modern workshop-based writing programs. They tend to be long on individual expression but dangerously short on canon and business acumen. These programs, particularly MFA programs, tend to dissolve into two-year excursions into privileged solipsism obscured by tendentious prose unmoored to the lodestars of a widely shared literary tradition.[4]

In other words, today's writing programs are great at teaching you how to craft a sonnet and weak at telling you that there's no market for sonnets.

The rise of self-publishing services distorts market signals about content quality, which then creates a false divide between self-published and conventionally published authors. Over the last decade, a new breed of very loud and very opinionated writers asserted that commercial publication is intrinsically flawed and that the only *real* way to be published is through self-publishing channels. They claim that self-publishing is easy and that anyone can do it and that more writers *should* self-publish because traditional publishers wouldn't know quality writing if it smacked them across the buttocks. The `r/SelfPublishing` subreddit is full of this kind of blind-faith advocacy for anything-goes publishing.

One subset of this group, full of libertarian piss and vinegar, thinks that self-publishing represents the next great epoch after Gutenberg. Their adherence to self-publishing channels is more ideological than economic. Another subset believes that they've got a First Amendment right to publish whatever they want, regardless of whether it's widely purchased, because commercial success is secondary to the imperative to "tell a good story." Yet another subset harbors resentment for their lack of commercial success so they've latched onto self-publishing as a redemptive pathway, thus protecting their pretensions of literary excellence from a reality check by the cruel marketplace. They're usually the ones who drip disdain for publishing executives.

All three of these groups have one thing in common: They don't really care about the finances. Which is good, because even though anyone can self-publish, almost no one makes money doing so.

Undoubtedly, self-publishing channels are useful and they serve a valuable purpose.[2] But self-publishing isn't *ipso facto* an exercise in literary heroism. People who assert that everyone "ought" to self-publish are generally the same folks who tried for years, and failed, to land a commercial publishing contract. While self-publishing offers a legitimate approach to publishing—and in some circumstances, depending on your goals, it may even be the optimal channel—when someone suggests that self-publishing is *intrinsically ideal*, it's likely that this person's advice is colored either by a libertarian mindset or by a history of personal disappointment.

2: Disclosure: I have self-published several erotica novellas (under pseudonym, of course) on Amazon. I'd never diminish the value of self-publishing or pretend that it's not a legitimate mode of communication. It certainly is!

For example, if you self-publish, you're guaranteed to have your book "out there," but if you believe in your book and think that both you and the book are destined for commercial greatness, then self-publishing means your audience will very likely be miniscule and your income will probably be something like 60 percent to 85 percent smaller than it otherwise would be, not counting your up-front investment to self-publish the book and to purchase copies for resale.[5]

Self-publishing isn't the albatross it once was, but if your aim is a national readership, you're disadvantaged if you lack conventional publishing credits. For some people with hyper-specific goals, self-publishing probably makes great sense. For others, it's the consolation prize for failing to write *good* books (i.e., books you revised in partnership with a freelance editor or a great critique group). The economics and the politics around self-publishing are too complex to distill it—as some do, loudly—as the purest and most virtuous mode of the art of writing.

Subsidy presses and content mills flood the online space with the seductive message that anyone can be an author and you can too for just $2,000 and/or 12 Easy Steps. People implicitly trust SERP—that is, the sequence of Search Engine Result Page scores that determine which websites appear in which order in Google and Bing. So when people type `how to be a published author` into their favorite search engine, they might judge individual results based on their apparent quality, but they almost never second-guess the message of those results considered collectively.

Traditional publishers and agents, because they're not in the business of cold-call recruiting, don't offer a ton of information about "how to be a published author." And the ones that do aren't trying to game Google for AdSense impression revenue.

You know who does play the game, though? Subsidy presses.

A subsidy press—usually called a *vanity press*—is a pay-to-publish organization.[3] Unlike a traditional publisher or an agent that waits for content to come to them, vanity presses actively recruit writers with elaborate tales about how they, too, can become published authors. Of course, these authors must pay the press for the privilege. It's not uncommon for authors to pay $2,000 or more for the equivalent of a conversion to

3: Some authorities maintain a distinction between a vanity publisher, a subsidy publisher, and a self-publishing support service, but because they all operate on a pay-to-publish model and extend similar services, I conflate them into a catch-all "pay to publish" rubric and use all of these terms interchangeably. From a typical author's perspective, the distinctions offer little practical difference.

PDF, a light proofread, a basic cover, a Facebook ad or two, and a modest initial print order.

Vanity presses send the message that it's perfectly normal for people to pay to get their books published. In fact, this message is so prevalent in some keyword searches that no reasonable writer could be faulted for thinking that pay-to-publish is the normal way to go. Vanities pay for ads on search-engine pages and they keyword-stuff specific terms on their webpages and blog entries so that people who know little about the industry are led to believe that most people find some "publisher" with whom they "cost-share" the production expenses. I've attended several author-sales events where it's clear that this pay-to-publish mindset is not only common, but considered ordinary.

To clarify: **Vanity. Publishing. Is. Not. Normal.**

There's an old rule: Authors sign checks on the back, not on the front. Although a small number of hyper-niche use cases justify a subsidy press, in general, people eager to publish a theoretically market-viable book should never use a pay-to-publish service.

And it's not just vanity presses that screw up search-engine results. A lot of the content mills that churn out substandard how-to articles clog the Web with stuff like "How to Publish a Book in 12 Easy Steps (with Pictures) (Updated for 2020)" and related nonsense. Sites like WikiHow or the old eHow Careers were the kings of 500-word articles stuffed with non-specific Pablum. They serve no useful purpose, but they do clutter SERP, vying with vanity presses to send an incoherent, and dangerously misleading, vision of what it means to be a published author.

Consider this gem from WikiHow, titled *How to Become a Published Writer*, in which the second step is "Learn the Art of Writing." You can't make this up:

> Major publishers are increasingly less willing to accept manuscripts with glaring grammatical errors, less-than-believable characters or poorly developed plots that get in the way of a potentially good story. To make sure you don't fall into any of these categories with your writing, take time to study the writing basics.

As of May 2020, this article was voted "100 percent helpful" by seven readers. It included 19 co-authors and earned nearly 115,000 page views. It offered four reader-supplied "success stories," including one person who said, "I think that this article helped me a lot. I am now an author."[6]

It's precisely this kind of irresponsible and outright misleading nonsense that emerging writers trust. And why shouldn't they? After all, *they Googled it*.

A Response to WikiHow

Contra WikiHow: (1) Authors cannot query major publishers directly. (2) The agents who work with major publishers aren't "increasingly less willing" to accept bad manuscripts—they've never been willing to accept them at all. (3) To land a contract with a major publisher, your writing must be several orders of magnitude above the level of "the writing basics."

Author Misperceptions

Some emerging authors bring two unhelpful mindsets to the table that, apart from industry foibles, adversely affect the start of their writing journey.

It's not true that "anyone can be a writer" if by *writer* we really mean *published author*. A whole litany of books and blogs—and don't forget National Novel Writing Month!—spread the dream that every single person nurtures a brilliant novel lying within, just waiting to debut to critical acclaim and financial success. The vast jungle of by-author-for-author blogs is so drenched with saccharine platitudes of writerly inspiration that just reading them for half an hour increases your risk of Type 2 diabetes by 17.2 percent.[4]

4: Trust me; I Googled it.

As far as hobbies go, writing is a deeply enriching one. And as a mode of therapy and self-diagnosis, it's beyond equal. By all means, keep a journal or spin short stories or poems in your free time. Submit them, even, to literary journals and anthologies.

But there's a huge difference between writing as a hobby versus writing novels intended for nationwide commercial consumption. A published author of the rank who attracts a line at a convention or a signing event isn't a random scribe plucked from obscurity and blessed with a book contract. Published authors with mid-to-large presses generally share three vital attributes: A significantly above-average cognitive profile (i.e., a high IQ[7] and high trait openness in the Big Five personality model[8]); a well-honed writing ability within the top one or two percentiles; and a deep network of critique partners, industry connections, and peer authors to supply the magic that others incorrectly label as *luck*.[5]

5: Although, in fairness, actual luck plays a much bigger role than people realize.

If you lack these three traits naturally, you're not doomed to failure. You just walk a different path. The best way to level-up an average cognitive profile, for example, is to read voraciously and spend a lot of time planning your work instead of just sitting down and writing blindly. The best way to overcome a mediocre writing ability is to write incessantly in partnership with a professional coach or a team of seasoned critique partners, while nurturing the humility to let their feedback meaningfully improve your style. The best way to address a weak network is to emerge from your cocoon and build a damned network.

The challenge I see over and over and over again is that perfectly average writers with a minimal network refuse to acknowledge that these attributes really do present a roadblock. So they take the approach that their first book, of which they're deeply proud,[6] is *inherently good*. Their lack of success, to them, sources somehow to nebulous industry or market forces. After all, they've read all sorts of inspiring stories about how writing every day leads to success and they knew a person whose NaNoWriMo novel got picked up by a small press somewhere.

6: Perhaps justifiably!

Writing novels with major presses is sort of like running a marathon. Anyone can do it, in theory, but in practice only an elite few pull it off. A lot of good writers aren't marathon runners—they settle into the groove of 10K runners who find some minor regional or niche-genre fame, or 5K runners who treat writing like a hobby and maybe sell a story every other year or so to a small-press anthology or literary journal. Almost no one completes a marathon the very first time they lace up their running shoes, however.

I believe—I truly believe—that *anyone can be a writer*. I also know that *some people can be published authors*. But deep experience has taught me that most emerging writers aren't willing to honestly assess their own gaps and then to spend the months or years to correct them. Instead, they shop their first novels, they refuse to network, they sometimes resort to self-publishing as a consolation prize, and they harbor a secret hope that someday the Success Fairy will pay them a visit.

Aspiring authors, I think, need both permission and active encouragement to spend time training before they sign up for a marathon. That so few get this message—that they think they *should* shop a first novel and they're a failure if they can't find an agent for it—contributes to so many unnecessarily crushed dreams.

Emerging authors often suffer from Jessica Fletcher Syndrome and assume that, as content creators, they're privileged stakeholders in the literary revenue cycle. Oh, *Murder, She Wrote*—that delightful TV series wherein Jessica Fletcher, played by the divine Angela Lansbury, worked by day as a mystery writer and by night as the crime-solving genius who single-handed solved the weekly murder epidemic in the otherwise placid Cabot Cove, Maine.

Lots of writers want to be Jessica Fletcher. They think the life of a full-time writer involves lots of airy writing time, intermixed with cocktail hours, tennis with friends, evening soirees, and grand public acclamation. So they develop this vision of an author as some sort of Public Artist of Great Repute™—a person whose creative prowess demands unstinting adulation from the community and abject deference from publishers and agents.

Some writers[7] believe (in part, perhaps, from bad advice derived from vanity-press websites) that authors are creative visionaries whose art is of paramount concern to the development of a book and whose satisfaction must be a top priority of editors and agents. Good gig, if you can get it, but the gig offers three caveats.

7: Usually, but not exclusively, of literary fiction.

First, authors don't earn a lot of money—a fact we'll review in detail in the next chapter. So unless you've got a sugar mama or a sugar daddy somewhere,[8] you're almost surely not going to give up your day job to write.

8: Better yet, one of each.

Second, authors exercise minuscule control over the book-development process. In a traditional publishing contract, authors don't get to pick covers or trim sizes or fonts or anything. They (mostly) control the words between "Chapter One" and "The End" and (mostly) nothing else. A book, as an artifact, is a product that's designed according to the marketing standards of the publisher. Authors rarely offer input into the structure or appearance of the final artifact, and sometimes they're contractually obligated to make changes to the text that don't meet the original "authorial intent." That's how the industry works.

Finally, authors do not receive creative deference from publishers or agents except ironically for tolerated-but-not-respected *artistes* with a big-enough platform to justify an ongoing business relationship despite the drama. In fact, authors who expect to be treated as customers or artists—rather than as suppliers of content—will find the process immensely frustrating. I once invoked an early-termination clause to cancel a contract for a book in progress, because that author's behavior toward editors was disruptively entitled, bordering on abusive. No one has time for a *prima donna.* Authors who approach their economic role with an author-as-supplier mindset rather than an author-as-customer mindset will find the process much less painful.

None of the preceding should suggest that authors aren't important. They are. But the industry as a whole doesn't really care about "authorial intent" or nurturing a quiet intellectual's life for writers—it cares about maximizing the first-quarter financial performance of a book.[9]

9: Almost no editorial leader will admit this truth publicly, however.

So don't expect to be treated like Jessica Fletcher, or to live like her. Yet if you align your thinking to the stakeholder web in the publishing industry, you might just find a low-drama, low-friction path that proves satisfying in the long run.

1.2 About This Book

These nine phenomena, when considered together, paint an unhappy picture. Authors lack recourse to well-considered advice about the industry and success pathways within it. Even when they try to learn in good faith, the quality of material out there—sometimes written by cranks or poseurs—often proves counterproductive when it's not merely blasé. And publishers lack the incentive to "train" people to be more effective submitters, because the current model offers a fairly clear demarcation to insiders about whom to accept or reject without having to spend a lot of time per submission.

Does all this commentary seem negative? Depressing? Snotty, even?

Lots of authorities encourage writers to perform certain generically helpful behaviors but relatively few encourage writers to *not do* certain characteristically counterproductive behaviors. Philosophically, the difference between a do versus a not-do approach is the difference between the *via positiva* and the *via negativa.* The universe of dangers that inadvertently harm authors' prospects is several orders of magnitude smaller than the universe of things that help them. As such, the focus in this book—as you saw in the foregoing section—is the *via negativa.* This thou-shalt-not approach isn't offered lightly, and certainly not in a spirit of hectoring sarcasm or condescension. Rather, this approach offers the biggest bang for the buck, by helping authors avoid the things that so often doom their peers to rejection slips.

Restated metaphorically: The *via positiva* tells you to "go north." Which is great, but context matters. If you rigidly chart a course of 0 degrees N, you'll likely fall off the cliff you didn't see coming because your nose remained in your compass as you painted-by-numbers your path to publication. The *via negativa*, by contrast, says, "don't steer more than 10 degrees east or west of north except to avoid the cliff, and by the way, avoid the cliff."[10] The *via negativa* doesn't guarantee you'll arrive unscathed at your destination, but it'll protect you from a lot of subtle harm on the journey that the warm-fuzzy positive approach never takes into account.

10: There's a world of difference between being told to "drive the speed limit" versus "don't exceed the speed limit," after all.

This book supports emerging authors who are curious about dipping their toes in the professional-author pool but who aren't sure how to get started and what sort of pitfalls they're likely to encounter early in the process. As such, the focus is on the practical side of writing long- and short-form fiction. We'll cover industry statistics, motivation clarification, book planning, and writers' groups. Actionable advice in the form of a get-fit-to-print program—modeled after a couch-to-5K program—level-sets expectations about how to get started, and a list of useful reference books points to good resources for the craft and business of writing.

Because of the literary focus of this volume, it cannot address common business questions about getting started. Different volumes in *The Diction Dude Essential Guides* series cover business structures, platform growth, and author marketing. A companion volume, *The Diction Dude Essential Guide to the Mechanics of Fiction*, covers the nuts-and-bolts of creative writing (although, again, from the *via negativa*).

This book assumes that the reader is interested in writing short stories or novels. We therefore won't cover non-fiction, work-for-hire content, or service journalism. In addition, there's not a ton of practical craft advice between these covers, apart from a collection of suggestions in Chapter 7. This framework is intentional, even if it appears a bit scattershot. Our goal here is to help you *get started*, from a professional perspective, to the point where you finally have a manuscript ready to shop. This volume won't help you get to the end point on your journey; it's focused on getting you through the first few milestones.

After all, those first few milestones are tough enough to achieve without cluttering your thinking with superfluous next-step advice that leave you stressing about next decade's writing goals!

1.3 Purpose of This Series

This volume is the first of ten. *The Diction Dude Essential Guides* series brings order out of the professional-writing chaos. Through 10 relatively short, focused volumes that cover significant topics about the craft and business of writing, readers will better understand the industry and optimal pathways through it.

Every coach brings a specific mental model to the game. The Diction Dude's bias is that it's best to be frank with authors by highlighting the things that very many writers consistently get wrong so that you may avoid those well-defined traps. You know, the *via negativa*. If you want nothing more than warm-fuzzy affirmation, go browse a by-author-for-author blog.

Because the Diction Dude has worked for more than two decades as a professional writer and editor, you'll enjoy a well-rounded approach given that your humble scribe has occupied just about every stakeholder position possible short of a luxury corner office in Manhattan. In fact, in no particular order, I've been—

- Published in several peer-reviewed professional markets
- Published in fiction and non-fiction anthologies
- A community-newspaper columnist
- A community-newspaper editorial leader—including a section editor, the paper's copy chief, and eventually the paper's editor in chief
- A freelance writer of short-form service journalism
- A freelance editor of online service journalism on behalf of several national media corporations, with a portfolio that's included editing thousands of different writers over the years
- The founder and CEO of a now-shuttered traditional micro-press that released more than a dozen books to market
- The founder of a multi-imprint small press with a distribution subsidiary
- Series editor of a genre-fiction anthology
- Publisher of a quarterly print journal of arts and letters
- Author of a well-performing series of pseudonymously self-published erotica novellas
- Board member of a non-profit writer's center—a role that included leading free monthly seminars about the business of writing
- Preceptor to a dozen for-credit academic interns
- Leader of a high-performing writers' group
- Speaker at local and regional writers' conferences

This broad diversity of experience means I'm better equipped than most to tell a nuanced story about the industry.[11] This series sources from those experiences. You won't find a series of "guaranteed to work" steps or insider shortcuts to publication.

11: I surely suffer blind spots of my own, of course.

One theory pervades this series, and in particular, this volume—that the most effective pathway to commercial success follows a deliberate approach to "leveling up" your work product by starting small, not being too hasty, and building a peer network. If your goal is to extract ancient secret kung-fu advice about how to cut to the top of the literary food chain without extra effort—well, good luck with that. Black swans exist, but if your business plan requires you to be one, the depth of your troubles exceeds this volume's capability to assist. This series offers a pathway that increases the likelihood of success, without guaranteeing it. *No one* can guarantee your success, but I will help you clear the deck of perhaps two-thirds of the most common obstacles that prevent emerging writers from earning an acceptance letter.

The 10 books in the series include:

- *The Diction Dude Essential Guide to Getting Started as a Professional Writer*: Optimized for people eager to write The Great American Novel, this volume surveys the literary publishing industry. It offers key statistics and prompts people to think about their goals in light of the different stakeholder pathways within the industry. The book includes a year-long Get Fit to Print framework that resembles a couch-to-5K program. It includes "50 informed suggestions" for novel-writing and practical advice about finding, and thriving within, a strong critique group.[12]

- ... *to the Mechanics of Fiction*: A companion to *Getting Started*, this volume addresses the most common errors in construction (and how to avoid them) in literary and genre fiction, plus tips for self-editing and manuscript formatting. It's focused on mechanics and technique.
- ... *to Character, Conflict, and Description*: Although *Mechanics of Fiction* touches on it, this volume dives more deeply into the ethical and psychological underpinnings of effective characterization. It assesses conflict holistically and as an essential partner to plot. It also offers best-practice advice for spinning descriptions and for building fictional universes.
- ... *to the Business of Writing*: A professional writer needs a business identity and an approach to winning contracts and selling books. This volume covers these essentials. It focuses on business structures for fiction authors, including brand identity and peer networking. Most authors don't like this green-eyeshade kind of stuff, but mastering it is key to demonstrating your worth to an agent or an acquisitions editor. This installment includes practical guidance for hand-selling your books at events and conventions.
- ... *to Querying and Market Diversification*: It's been said that most authors spend 1,000 hours drafting their novels and 1 minute drafting their query package. This volume explores markets and queries—how to find the right market and how to fine-tune a pitch to meet editors' and agents' expectations. It also addresses the relative strengths and weaknesses of each of the four primary publishing models.
- ... *to Growing a Platform*: Most authors *must* be marketing gurus, regardless of whether you self-publish or work through a major New York imprint. Building a platform and harnessing that platform to sell books is hard. Without it, your attractiveness to commercial publishing partners declines substantially. In this volume, we cover the marketing angle, from growing a fanbase to motivating your readers to buy your next book.
- ... *to the Literary Revenue Cycle*: All of book publishing follows two intertwined pathways. One, the literary road, views a manuscript from drafting to production to release to retirement from backlist. The other, the financial road, considers the best risk-mitigation and cost-effectiveness strategies as a book as a literary artifact progresses from ideation to execution to retirement. This volume explores the major touchstones in the life of a book, from its drafting to its removal from catalogs, from both the economic and the editorial perspectives. You'll see how the sausage gets made in ways that most authors—even self-published ones—never experience, and you'll understand how the almighty profit-and-loss estimate explains your last rejection letter even if you pitched a perfect query.
- ... *to Self-Publishing Excellence*: Lots of resources tell you how to self-publish your book, but this one's the only book that shows you the tricks of the trade from a small-press publisher's point of view. It includes ample advanced tips about formatting and collaborative

12: This book. The one you're holding.

editing to make your life easier, too.

- ... *to Service Journalism*: Many authors who write for income focus not on fiction but on technical non-fiction. Common work includes copywriting, document editing, writing how-to articles for websites, and developing supplemental material for print magazines. This volume explores the world of writing and editing for profit in a short-form, non-fiction space. It's a much different beast from fiction writing, but with a good hustle, it pays far better in the long run.
- ... *to Persuasive Writing*: Essays and opinion columns make great fodder for newspapers or for blogs, but short-form persuasive commentary is harder to pull off than it looks. This volume looks at the structures of persuasive essays and creative non-fiction and outlines the basics of critical reasoning required to generate convincing arguments in a limited amount of space.

This series, and the 10 targeted volumes within it, are written with love. May they help you on your journey as you find your voice, hone your craft, and join your tribe.

2 Expectations

Many authors seek to share their stories with a broad audience. However, the publishing industry must maximize revenue from wholesale book buyers by promoting saleable stories that are likely to at least break even in the open market. Even though a story might be a good one, effective storytelling alone isn't enough to ensure adequate market reach. From an author's perspective, therefore, publishing sometimes proves frustrating because the mismatch of publisher and author goals leads to conflict. So we explore the state of today's publishing industry, but also the rich depths of your personal aspiration to be a published author. Your personal "why" colors your "how" in several important but non-obvious respects.

2.1 The Journey to Ten Percent

AUTHORS OFTEN SEEK PUBLICATION. Queries to small presses and literary agents offer the typical context for traditional publishing agreements. Yet acceptance rates for most emerging authors remain vanishingly small. So how do people actually break into their first literary contract?

A lot of material has crossed my desk over the years. With probably 75 percent of it, I conclude within the first 100 words that the piece remains a functional first draft and read no further. Maybe another 5 percent is decent, from a technical perspective, but not a good fit with the market's clearly expressed editorial vision. Add another 15 percent for stuff that failed to materially conform to the submission guidelines and so isn't even eligible for review. That leaves about 5 percent of the slush pile to be evaluated primarily on its literary merit.

Most markets accept only a tiny fraction of inbound pitches. Prestige markets may contract with less than a hundredth of a percent of submitters, while less-selective or niche presses might creep closer to 2 percent or 3 percent.

These statistics aren't off the cuff, either. At the micro-press I co-founded and ran for five years, we coded every declined submission with a primary-rejection category. We knew exactly why we passed on a pitch. And it's true that only 5 percent of submissions warrant a meaningful review of the query package. And even then, acceptance is a crapshoot. Our rate hovered a hair below 1 percent, and we were much less selective than many of our peers.

Observing that a given market averages a 1 percent acceptance rate doesn't mean that any given author enjoys an equal a one-in-a-hundred shot, however. A skilled writer with an extensive portfolio might eventually build a personal acceptance rate of 10 percent or better, whereas an emerging writer with no portfolio, no experience, no special talent, and no network may see a lifetime acceptance rate of effectively 0 percent.

Bridging the gap between the Zero Percenters and Ten Percenters is hard, but doable. Most authors who drown in the proverbial ream of rejection slips fall into one of two camps, both of which are occupied by unrepentant Zero Percenters.

The first consists of people who prowl as literary lone wolves. In many cases, the underlying story shows real promise but it's not obvious from the query package that the writers fine-tuned a piece with a high-functioning critique group or through the services of an independent book editor. They're doomed by a litany of obvious and avoidable errors, and they're often not open to feedback about the comparative quality of either their story or their technique. Their chief problem is *literary quality*.

The other consists of folks who've grown calloused to rejection. Many of these people aren't even inherently bad writers—rather, they're hobbled by a profound lack of understanding about the economic dynamics of the market. This is the group most likely to target the wrong piece to the wrong place with casual disregard for each agent's or publisher's unique set of editorial guidelines. It's also the group that insists on shopping manuscripts that, because they stray far afield of genre norms, will almost never find a receptive audience. Their chief problem is *market viability*.

For both groups, a hard but achievable path rescues them from Zero Percenter territory. This book charts a course for the first mile or so of that journey.

Authors love their work. They're deeply invested in their stories. Yet if we were uniformly good judges of the things we love, then rejection letters would not exist. Neither would divorces. So when a person writes a *magnum opus* and it fails to get any interest at all, some of these authors either descend into cynicism or they give up their dream.

Misaligned expectations, more than any other factor, contribute to the breakdown of the relationships among authors, editors, and agents, starting from the moment of querying. And this misalignment sources from many tainted springs—it's not just inexperienced authors who are at fault. Editors and agents play a role, too; I wasn't a perfect small-press leader and I certainly committed my fair share of mistakes of both tone and substance.

But even though acceptances are rare, they're not impossible. When you grasp the point of publishing and the numbers undergirding the industry, you're well on your way to setting reasonable expectations for yourself—and for potential publishing partners. Even the mistake-prone ones. That knowledge offers a breadcrumb trail for moving from a Zero Percenter to a Ten Percenter.

2.2 The Point of Publishing

The most significant misunderstanding that emerging authors bring to the traditional-publishing cycle relates to the nature and purpose of the broad financial and editorial processes that make the creaky wheels of the industry turn.

Five points here.

First, *the point of publishing is to generate profit for publishers*. Period. Full stop. End of discussion.

It's not to celebrate great literature or to highlight the next generation of powerful voices or to bestow wealth and happiness for authors and poets, despite the mellifluous platitudes comprising the mission statements of publishing companies across the big blue marble. Publishing is a business, albeit an odd one—publishers make their money selling products that contain the intellectual property of authors from whom they license that work. If a publisher thinks a project isn't likely to generate money, it won't be published. Conversely, if a publisher thinks a project *will* generate money, a poor-quality manuscript isn't intrinsically a barrier to contracting.[1]

1: Admittedly, additional nuance accrues to not-for-profit or college-affiliated publishers, which operate under different economic pressures from commercial for-profit presses—but in most cases, editorial decision-making approaches don't appreciably differ.

Second, don't overlook the significance of the clause *from whom they license that work*. Lots of books enter the global market each year—roughly 300,000 or so from traditional presses of all sizes, in all genres and markets and languages—but very many more pitches than that cross publishers' desks in an average year. A very large number of authors compete for a comparatively small number of book contracts. From a purely economic perspective, then, authors function not as left-brain creators, but as suppliers of raw materials[2] in an oversaturated market where the natural result is a depression of supplier revenue and an increase in baseline quality standards to be considered as a supplier of good repute. The process of vetting manuscripts, called *gatekeeping*, is the reason that agents and queries function as middleman roadblocks: A literary expert in the form of an agent or an acquisitions editor must assess and endorse whether a given pitch by a given author makes for a culturally and economically satisfactory supplier relationship.

2: Manuscripts!

Third, incoherent market signals mean that figuring out the right kind of product is the devilry that dare not speak its name. In many industries, business leaders perform focus groups or run A/B tests or otherwise hone the optimal product at the optimal price to generate optimal revenue. In publishing, not so much. The book-buying market is notoriously fickle and impossible to predict. People enjoy the sparkly vampire stories until they don't. They consume period fantasy until they don't. Tools like profit-and-loss statements guesstimate whether a given book might perform well in the market. But the truth is, no one knows until after it's released how any specific book will perform. This ambiguity tends to make acquisitions editors conservative in their contracting strategies. That's why it's harder for emerging authors, or authors of genre-bending works, to find a receptive audience. No major player is eager to be the first to take a risk on a new supplier of hard-to-market content.

Fourth, the people who buy books from retailers tend to form relationships with authors, not with publishers. Lots of people loved the Harry Potter series, for example, and stood in line to get a signing with J.K. Rowling, but almost none of them knew that Scholastic published that series;[3] their love for the boy wizard didn't magically translate into sales for other Scholastic authors. That's why the idea of *platform*—of authors growing their own fan base—is so important in contracting conversations. An author who can bring 1,200 high-probability sales leads to the table who will buy her book in the first calendar quarter is

3: In the U.S., anyway. Bloomsbury Publishing controlled the market in the United Kingdom.

a more attractive business prospect than one who brings a dozen. An author's built-in audience mitigates the publisher's risk arising from the inherent fuzziness of profit-and-loss estimates and market predictions.

Fifth, books are expensive. The cost to produce a book at a small- or mid-sized press can run from $10,000 to $50,000 or more[4] —and that's not counting author advances or large print runs. A major release by a major press might incur total project costs well north of $1 million. If a book succeeds, everyone wins: the publisher, the author, the agent, the retailers, the distributors. When a book fails, *only the publisher* incurs the loss. So the publisher has an incentive, especially in light of the incoherent market signals, to minimize its financial risk. There's a maxim among publishers: One blockbuster subsidizes 99 other failed books. It's an exaggeration but not by much, given that most books do indeed fail (at least financially) but losses are recouped in the aggregate by the very small numbers of books that hit the bestseller lists.

4: Assuming fair-market accounting. A micro press operating in the grey zone of "free" labor supplied by the press owners often spends less than $500 in total direct cash outlays, but without any meaningful advertising and distribution push for the final product.

Overlaying this complexity, two additional phenomena disrupt this rickety industry with all the bemused malevolence of a bored cat dancing upon a shelf of porcelain figurines.

On one hand, self-publishing models eliminate publishers and distributors altogether, so only the author bears the financial risk and reward of publication. Yet the corresponding lack of professional editorial gatekeeping means that very many self-published books enter the market without the type of quality-control checking that's *de rigueur* with traditional presses. And because 70 percent of new books are self-published, the distorted signal-to-noise ratio means that all books become harder to discover even as significantly more books compete for the same amount of annual sales dollars.

On the other hand, subsidy-publishing models work great for those subsidy presses but the author generally bleeds cash through the nose for a book that at least looks better (usually) than a typical self-published title but still doesn't enjoy meaningful sales-and-distribution opportunity.

So the industry is chaotic and cutthroat, with conflicting models that makes uniformity of industry standards well-nigh impossible.

If you're not yet depressed, just wait. We're about to dive in to the statistics.

2.3 State of the Industry

Consider these facts:

- The U.S. Census Bureau reports that for 2017, SIC Code 51113 (book publishers) featured nearly 2,100 firms of all sizes employing almost 72,000 people, for a payroll of nearly $5.7 billion against preliminary estimated receipts of $28.8 billion.[9] For context, those receipts—if you doubled them—would still be less than Apple's 2018 annual *profit*.

- As of 2016, there's now roughly 1 million books published annually (70 percent of them are self-published), with an additional 13 million available in back catalogs. Any given print book selected at random (i.e., the ISBN is drawn from a hat) enjoys a less than 1 percent probability of ever having been stocked in a bricks-and-mortar retail environment.[10]
- A print book released by a major publisher will sell, on average, 10k to 12k copies, but there's significant variation in sales totals depending on the author, the press and the quantity of the author's previously published books.[12] For example, sales for 2015 Man Booker Prize nominees ranged from 20,102 to 1,008.[13]
- A 2014 U.K. survey found that one-third of published authors make less than $500 per year from their writing; the median income for full-time pro writers was less than $15,000.[11]
- The 2018 Authors Guild author-income survey tallied results from 5,100 respondents. Of these, 53 percent write full-time. For all respondents, 46 percent are exclusively traditionally published; 27 percent are exclusively self-published; the remainder have used both models. The median annual income for full-time traditionally published writers related to their book-specific activities was just $12,400. The median income of *all* surveyed authors for all writing-related activities was $6,080. A whopping 25 percent of all surveyed authors earned $0 in book-related income in 2017. Self-published authors earned 58 percent less on average than their traditionally published counterparts.[3]

A Note about the AG Survey

To be a member of Authors Guild, you must already be an author of more than one publication with baseline sales or circulation exposure—so those stats don't include many tens of thousands of self-published authors who don't even qualify for AG membership yet spend their summer weekends selling their self-published books, one at a time, at author meet-ups at rural craft shows or art festivals. This survey includes AG members as well as members of several professional genre-writing groups with different membership standards, but the point stands. If the stats included a representative sample of all hobbyist writers schlepping one or two self-published books, the results would skew far worse than they already do.

- The 2019 Diversity Baseline Survey report from Lee & Low Books, co-authored by Laura M. Jiménez and Betsy Beckert of Boston University, suggests that the industry overall is 75 percent white, 75 percent female, 82 percent heterosexual, and 89 percent non-disabled.[14] These race and disability numbers are in line with U.S. Census estimates, but the industry is significantly more female and non-heterosexual than the country as a whole. Relatedly, although firm numbers aren't available, evidence from sources including *The New York Times* suggest that independent booksellers overwhelmingly lean progressive in staffing if not always in public-facing programming.[15] The OpenSecrets.org database reveals that for the 2016 U.S. election cycle, the Printing & Publishing industry donated $13.47 million to Democrats and $3.29 million to Republicans, a roughly 4-to-1 ratio. In the 2018 cycle, the same industry has donated $16.47 million to Democrats and $2.43 million to Republicans—a nearly 6.8-to-1 ratio. As recently as 2000, the donations were roughly even at roughly $3.1 million apiece. The phenomenon of *cancel culture*—where progressive activists get fired up on Twitter and publishing executives cave—is a real thing that, in 2019, led to several books being withdrawn or deprioritized under questionable circumstances.[16] The effect on right-of-center readers and writers hasn't been explored.

Depressed yet?

Here's the thing about publishing: You won't strike it rich. Author-income graphs are the ultimate hockey-stick curves: More than half the population of writers makes $0 while a handful of nationally known, traditionally published writers earn $300,000 or more. Resist the delusion that you're America's Next Top Author—a successor to E.L. James or J.K. Rowling—just waiting to be plucked from obscurity through your debut novel and thereby become a millionaire. You know why "we all know" these famous debut novelists? *Because they're so rare, globally and across the last two decades, that we can count them on our fingers with digits to spare.*

But if being an author weren't tough enough, the industry itself continues to thrash in paroxysms of agony fueled in large part by the smiley, soulless phenomenon of Amazon.

2.4 Amazon as Disruptor

The story of Amazon is a tale of dominos tipping around a very big room like a giant Rube Goldberg machine, shredding everything in its path with a speed and ferocity so mesmerizing that you forget to be terrified by it until you realize that Humpty ain't ever gettin' put back together so you might as well snag free two-day shipping in recompense. Early Amazon—back when it was *just* a big online bookstore—originally disrupted retail. When there was plenty of room for indie bookstores and chains to coexist, Amazon did three things differently that brought the complacent book-retail market to its knees.

First, it effectively opened the wholesale distribution catalogs to the book-buying market, so Amazon wasn't constrained by the number of linear feet of shelf space it offered. Why browse a bookstore with 50,000 books curated by human buyers whose taste may differ from yours, when you could keyword search for specific books among an inventory of 5 million and get exactly what you want, delivered to your front door? Without you even having to don thy pantaloons?

Second, Amazon put significant price pressures on the market. Its most significant contribution was the heavy promotion of e-books, which don't require inventory space and could be priced low enough to eat into physical sales, especially when the company practically gave away Kindles. You can't buy e-books, by the way, from the local bricks-and-mortar retail shop. Publishing expert Jane Friedman, writing in 2017, noted that Amazon published (from its own imprint) eight of the top 20

Kindle sellers of 2016 and accounts for 50 percent of the national sales pie for print book sales.[17] That's not insignificant.

Third, by democratizing publishing through its CreateSpace program, which removed the time-honored gatekeeping function performed by agents and publishers, a deluge of new self-published books drowned the market. Most were awful, but that wasn't the point. A large-enough segment of readers with a constrained-enough budget proved willing to take a chance on free or cheap e-books penned by self-published authors, thus draining revenue from traditional publishers, their distribution networks, and their retail partners.

The net result? First, bookstores closed—mostly indies, but including chains like Borders. Too much of their traffic shifted away from the physical retail space and into the world of Amazon Prime. Even bookstores that tried to keep up by differentiating themselves tended to fail because so much of the differentiation didn't effectively matter. A friend of mine, who once owned a small bookstore, lamented people walking in, finding books they liked, then ordering them on their phone on Amazon before walking out without having made a single in-store purchase (but often, enjoying a cup of "free" coffee).[5]

5: That said, when many indie bookstores stopped at least pretending to be open to all customers and started catering to progressive patrons with #Resist mindsets, they didn't really help their own economic viability and brand loyalty. It's unclear *who* thought it was a great survival strategy for indie bookstores to give half their potential customer base the middle finger, but bless their hearts, so many followed that path.

Next to fall were the distribution networks feeding books from publishers to retailers. With fewer retailers, the distribution segment started to implode. In fact, in early 2019, Baker & Taylor started winding down, a major loss given that already-strapped bookstores enjoy fewer (and thus, less competitive) options for buying books.

And with fewer distributors still eager to earn yesteryear's gross-margin targets, the cost of getting new books into the distribution system for small presses shot up. In some cases, getting a new book into distribution costs several hundred dollars per title, with ongoing fees on top of it as well as a laughably absurd slice of net revenue—never mind that you'd have to enter books into several distribution catalogs simultaneously to effectively cover a big-enough chunk of the retail market. A small press would have to sell hundreds of books just to make up the cost of being in the network. And not to put too fine a point on it, but most micro press books don't sell hundreds of copies. A thousand-copy sales history is well-nigh miraculous.

As such, many of the smallest presses content themselves to distribute through Ingram—the only major national distributor left, and something of a large and undifferentiated Dumpster fire in its own right—even though there are so many books in the Ingram catalog that almost no small-press title will ever rise to the level of a commercial buyer's attention. At least, not without paying Ingram hundreds of dollars in ad fees or earning sweat equity with local indie booksellers.

With distribution for the smallest presses effectively no different from distribution for self-published authors, it ought not to surprise anyone that a typical small-press title struggles to sell even a tenth of what a major press sells, *vis-a-vis* any random title. That anemic performance means most authors enjoy no advances and almost no royalty payments, and even the small presses themselves are collapsing at a fierce rate (*q.v.*, Authors Guild survey).

But because Amazon is a publisher and a retailer and a distributor all in one big roof, its profit margins, thin as they are, outperform others in the industry that do not enjoy the benefit of massive vertical integration.

But hey, authors—at least you nibble with gratitude at the scraps of free two-day shipping chucked in your direction by the behemoth that effectively gutted the industry you're so desperately eager to join.[6]

6: Your writing prompt for tomorrow? *Stockholm Syndrome.*

2.5 Impelled to Write

Given these statistics about the industry, it's perhaps understandable to indulge in a bit of existential despair. Publishing is a high-cost, low-margin business wherein the supply of raw materials (your stories!) far outpaces the industry's own demand for output. And even if you manage to land a contract—and the odds are strongly against you—you're probably not going to make enough money to quit your day job, or even go part time, from novel-writing alone. So why bother?

We bother because it's important! It's a myth that the point of writing is to be published. *Writing* and *publishing* aren't synonyms. A writer who never seeks publication is no less a writer than the prolifically published Stephen King or Duane Patterson or Sue Grafton.

Writing, fundamentally, distills to a love of the craft and the discipline to advance it, story by story. If you write, and you enjoy it, and you continue to sharpen your skills, then *you are a writer*. Compose novels all day long and simply file them in a cabinet somewhere. No law requires that you seek to publish what you draft. In fact, writing for the sake of it frees you from the constraints of strict genre conformance and all the related rules that chafe so many emerging writers and poets. If you love to tell stories and don't care to ever sign a contract, then write whatever you want, whenever you want. You'll be a better person for it.

That being said, not all people who write, or even get published, love the craft. The best example of this kind of writer is the professional in some industry who determines that having a book on the market legitimizes his or her product-and-service portfolio or enhances credibility on the professional speakers' circuit. And for some people—especially non-academic technical writers—writing is less about the craft than it is about the output.

That's okay, too.

Your task, antecedent to any other activity before you launch your writing career, is first to reflect on the reason you want to be a writer.

What about writing satisfies you? Is it the discipline of sitting down, day after day, crafting words into a narrative that tells a story? Do you delight in self-editing? Do you enjoy developing characters, or inventing universes, or plumbing the depths of the human experience?

Conversely: Do you hate writing but see it as a necessary component in service to a broader goal?

The reason you need to think through what you value is because if your primary satisfaction comes from sitting by yourself, crafting characters and scenarios and universes, then you understand something important about your point of origin on your authorial journey. If you hate the drudgery of editing and you're not comfortable sharing your work with a critique group, and the thought of actually *marketing* your story to strangers makes your anxiety peak higher than Mt. Everest, then perhaps publication shouldn't be a part of your near-term future.

You don't need to be published to thrive as a writer. If the craft of writing is what keeps you at it, then by all means, keep crafting. Writing for yourself doesn't make you any less of a writer. This point matters, because there's a world of difference between authors who thrive commercially and writers who endure publication because they hate it but nevertheless feel like they must.

So ask yourself more questions: Do you get excited about the prospect of reading your work in front of dozens or hundreds of strangers? Are you thrilled with the thought of spending perhaps up to half of your "writing time" focused not on writing but on growing a social-media platform? Are you prepared to have the word-baby you midwifed over many long months or years suddenly smacked on its backside by an editor you've likely never met and who might not be a specialist in your genre? Are you okay knowing that, to be a typical writer, you probably won't get any nibbles until your fourth, fifth or sixth completed manuscript?

Only if you're a touch masochistic will you thrive in the contemporary commercial-publishing marketplace. For everyone else, just write. It's the little moments of creative joy, and not book contracts, that validate you.

2.6 Authorial Motivations

The "why" question around your instinct to write directly addresses both whether, and how, you ought to pursue publication. Most importantly, the "why" question leads you to an answer, unique to you, of what it means to be successful. If developing bold new worlds and characters is all the reward you need, then don't distract yourself from your success by the almost certainly painful process of publishing. *Just write.* If you want to share your stories, post them to a blog.

If, however, you really believe that success includes a book available on the open market, then your plan for writing must sync with this objective. For starters, you'll approach writing differently. It's no longer a question of what you want to write, but rather of what you want to sell.

And when you think of what—or if!—you want to sell, consider where you fit in.

The Social Author It's not unusual for a hobbyist author not seeking publication to nevertheless advance in fits and starts toward publication. This profile is common, for example, in communities with strong local regions for National Novel Writing Month—where people get together in-person every November to write 50,000 words.

Have fun. Nurture your inner scribe. Make friends. If you treat it like a serious hobby, you'll probably eventually develop at least a few short stories or poems that your critique group can help work into reasonable shape. In the short run, don't think about publication. When the "maybe I should shop something" voice incessantly whispers sweet nothings in your ear, only then should you think about what parts of your slush pile might be saleable. Until then, don't fret. Hone your craft. Thrive in your local community. You enjoy something special that many people never experience, so treasure it while it lasts.

The One-Book Wonder One-book authors are generally folks who've got one major project in them. Maybe it's a family history, or this one super-cool detective story, or a stand-alone fantasy epic, or an in-depth treatise about a specific shipwreck on Lake Superior. Regardless, the writer completed one project and really doesn't have fire in the belly—at least in the near future—to start another book.

This person might struggle to build the infrastructure to pursue commercial success for just one item of work product, and some agents might resist taking on an author who will, automatically, not be receptive to follow-up contracts if the book performs well.

One-book authors should not expect industry accolades and bountiful piles of literary cash raining down upon them. Instead, a self-publish scenario is probably the best solution—it's cheap, it's (relatively) easy, and you'll have the print artifact you can sell or give to friends and family and perhaps promote at occasional author meet-ups. Don't tell yourself that self-publishing is bad. For one-book wonders, it's an almost ideal win-win outcome.

Self Publishing Isn't Bad

The stigma that used to stink up self-published authors like Great Aunt Ethel's perfume cabinet has long since dissipated thanks to the sweet, refreshing breeze of popular authors also electing to occasionally self-publish new books. A few elderly editors in New York may still disdain self-published writers, but that bias industry-wide has mostly gone away. Of course, people still judge *bad* self-published books, but no one nowadays assumes that a self-published author is *therefore* a bad author. Too many hyper-niche books of genuine literary merit but insufficient market viability have in recent years to testified to the truth of the new publishing model. The only catch is that going all-in on the self-published model for several books sometimes erects barriers to future commercial contracts.

That said, there's still a (very much justified) bias against pay-to-publish authors.

The Multi-Book Author Whether it's through loyalty to a specific genre or a character series or a theme, some people write and write and write. This kind of author can be the most appealing to publishers and agents—if the writer has chops and achieves reasonable market success early on, then that author is a good investment for future book contracts—but the author really has to focus on a specific market and genre to thrive, and woe betide he who cheats on a genre-based fan club.

Multi-book authors really must focus on platform building. No way around it. You'll have to do events and trade shows and newsletters and social media and a blog and, and, and, and, and. All of which cuts into your writing time!

Furthermore, mid-list—that segment of reliable, prolific authors who weren't really household names but nevertheless at least broke even-ish for their publishers—is drying up. It's harder to be a multi-book author with mid-to-large presses unless you're willing to really dive into alternative forms of monetized self promotion, including potentially merchandise, podcasting, and paid speaking or newsletter gigs. There's no future in mid-list anymore.

A tip for the novice who aspires to be a multi-book author: Write a book. Then another. Then another. Don't think about publication until you've personally verified that you can write good stuff (as adjudged by competent peers!) on a tight schedule while building a platform, not alienating your editor, and avoiding alcoholism. Despite the widespread romantic visions of a gentle literary life filled with sunshine, word counts, wine spritzers, and award dinners—Jessica Fletcher Syndrome—professional writing is neither an easy nor a profitable career. Really, it's not. Until you hit your stride after several years (decades?) of apprenticeship and the appropriate alignment of the stars, on an hourly basis it's more lucrative to ask people if they want fries with that instead of whether they want an autograph on the title page.

However, multi-book authors who self-publish and aren't looking for significant revenue or literary exposure but rather crave being creative and meeting fellow writers—well, these people often thrive.

The Author Who Writes to Support a Career For some people, book-length writing is an adjunct to some other career. College faculty, for example, sometimes operate in a publish-or-perish world where tenure is dependent on publication history. Some professionals, especially consultants and full-time motivational speakers, publish books (sometimes, admittedly, penned by ghostwriters) to serve as a professional legitimizer. None of this rationale is bad, but for them the act of writing is less a function of the joy of the craft and more a desire for the credibility that a book implies.

A word of caution: Non-fiction business books are a dime a dozen, but getting a contract generally requires 10,000 Twitter followers. You can sometimes get away in genre fiction with no platform in the self-published e-book space, but unless you self-publish your business book, you'll find it hard to get a non-fiction business- or leadership-focused book contract without a significant, active, monetizable social media or mailing-list roster.

The Author Who Writes as a Career Lots of people work full-time as writers, but their writing isn't necessarily fiction work. As the Authors Guild survey notes, annual revenue for full-time authors presents a wickedly steep curve. You have to already have "made it" to make it financially—and even then, your life will be a hustle.

But dive into that survey and you'll note some careful use of language. There's a difference between book-related income vs. writing-related income, for example. Book-related income relates primarily to royalties or sales; writing-related income includes honoraria for speaking gigs.

Very few working authors, apart from authors whose economic needs are satisfied by a spouse or a trust fund or a sugar parent, enjoy the luxury of a daily routine focused on personal writing divorced from any need to pay the monthly AmEx bill. Most perform other work that smooths the irregularities in an author's personal revenue stream or offers stuff like insurance and retirement benefits.

For a great case in point, look up the blog of the charming Jim C. Hines, a Michigan author of speculative fiction and the publisher of a quarterly-ish newsletter by a goblin named Klud. Every year, he publishes a detailed personal author-earnings report—a must-read insight into how he does it and how his income fluctuations on contract cycles.

2.7 Industry Q&A

Bits and pieces of the publishing world take emerging writers by surprise. I've pulled together a short Q&A section to address a few high-level points that frequently arise with aspiring authors.

What are the primary publishing models? The industry tracks four different publishing models. The first is self-publishing, where the author manages book production, distribution, and retail sales through marketplaces like Amazon, Lulu, or Xlibris. The next is traditional publishing, where a publishing company prepares an author's manuscript that meets its editorial and financial targets, then manages its sales and distribution on the authors' behalf. The third is subsidy publishing—sometimes called *vanity publishing*—where the author pays a company to prepare and produce a book regardless of its relative editorial or financial viability. The fourth is hybrid publishing, where an author pays the publisher to prepare and distribute the book, but the publisher only accepts books that meet baseline standards of editorial quality. Check out the forthcoming *The Diction Dude Essential Guide to Self-Publishing Excellence* for a detailed framework for managing your own books and *The Diction Dude Essential Guide to Querying and Market Diversification* for a more in-depth review of the four models.

Should I have an agent? Yes. Agents are required for access to mid-to-large publishing companies (they're much less common with small presses). You can get published without an agent in the small-to-mid-sized press space, but it's generally better to have one. However, short-fiction anthologies and most literary journals aren't agented markets, so if you only shop short stuff, an agent isn't necessary.

How do I get an agent? Agents and small-press editors are the only facets of the market open to cold querying from unrepresented authors. To land an agent, you must find one—the annual *Agent's Market* book is a good research starting point—and go from there. Look for agents who are members of the Association of Author Representatives and who do not charge fees to review manuscripts. Similarly, seek agents who specialize in your genre. It's not true that "any" agent is a good agent. Agents new to the industry working in obscure agencies may prove effectively useless because they're not well-known among the elite acquisitions editors. However, they're quicker to nibble on emerging talent. Veteran, well-connected agents are much harder to land, and sometimes only open the door to you by word-of-mouth connections with authors already on their list.

What does an agent cost? Agents shouldn't charge any up-front fees. Rather, they earn a percentage of author earnings (often 20 percent for domestic royalties). Agents receive compensation from the publisher, remove their cut, and then forward the balance to the writers. Thus, you can't stiff your agent.

Do I need a business structure? Always consult with your attorney and your certified public accountant for specific advice. In general, however, part-time authors of short fiction and genre-fiction novels generally do not establish corporate entities, although some elect to establish a sole proprietorship. That calculus may change based on the relative risk of the work being produced and on the specific tax implications for your revenue and, as relevant, sales strategy.[7]

7: See Chapter 8 for additional context.

Do I need insurance? Speak to an insurance broker in your community for specific guidance. Usually, fiction writers do not insure themselves unless they're writing some forms of memoir or unauthorized biography. Often, professional writers in industries and genres where litigation is more frequent tend to obtain coverage to protect themselves against lawsuits.

What's a valid use case for pay-to-publish companies? A subsidy press makes sense for people who have one non-market-viable book in them and they have more money than time to execute on a book project. For example, a church that produces a cookbook for its 100th anniversary may well find value in working with a subsidy press. However, authors who aspire to release several novels to market should avoid subsidy presses. Many traditional presses evaluate your publication history and the presence of a vanity press in the mix raises a serious red flag about your professional comportment.

How much should I pay to "cost share" with a publisher? Nothing. The language of "cost sharing" is a red flag that a publisher is attempting to obscure its pay-to-publish business model. A legitimate vanity press (and they do exist) doesn't sugar-coat the transaction: You're paying to publish a book that's otherwise not viable in the open market. In principle, there's nothing intrinsically shady about that process. When publishers blow smoke about "telling great stories" and that all the writer needs to do is "share the cost" of development and release and marketing, they're preying on a segment of the market that doesn't understand the range of publishing business models. Put differently: Publishers don't "cost share." That's a euphemism for *pay to publish*—and legitimate subsidy presses need not be opaque about what they're doing.

What's a "hybrid" publisher? A hybrid publisher is a publisher that exercises normal editorial gatekeeping—i.e., it works through queries—but charges fees to the author to bring the book to market on the theory that the editorial quality of the project is good but the book doesn't enjoy an expected positive return in expected sales. Hybrids are relatively new, and some subsidy presses have maliciously claimed the hybrid label to further confuse readers. A subsidy press will publish anything as long as the check clears. A hybrid press only publishes material of genuine literary merit, and it offers the normal mix of editorial services including substantive editing and cover design, but it makes up for the lack of market viability by passing its production costs to the author. In theory, a hybrid press makes a great opportunity for highly skilled emerging writers with the financial flex to support their book's development. In practice, the model is new enough, and subsidy presses have sufficiently muddied the waters, that swimming in this market segment proves treacherous.[8]

8: The Diction Dude's sister company, Lakeshore Literary, includes a hybrid-publishing imprint, *Lakeshore Hybrid*.

How much money can I realistically make as an author? It's true that a few black swans earn millions of dollars as writers. However, most full-time authors earn less than $10,000 annually.[3] Do not become a writer with the expectation that you'll earn a decent living out-of-the-gate. *You will not*. It takes many years and a certain degree of luck to make even a minimum-wage income, annualized, although income from writing-adjacent activities sometimes helps.

Do I need a professional editor? Maybe. An independent book editor helps emerging writers level-set their expectations about the structural and syntactical quality of their book. They're often expensive, however. As a weakly generalized rule, the smaller the press the less you'll need to worry about hyper-precise writing, because many of the micro press editors either lack the skill to edit well or because they elect to work with emerging talent even if the talent presents as a fixer-upper. However, a manuscript that's never been vetted by a high-performing group will absolutely benefit from a pass or two from a contracted book editor before you look for an agent. Seek a professional contract editor who offers a first-chapter critique at lower cost so you're better able to calibrate your expectations and the editor's relative skill.

What's the difference between a small press and a large press? Large presses enjoy a large sales force to help get promising new releases into bookstores across the planet. However, your book must meet a very specific profile—rock-solid writing and clear market value—before it'll even be considered by large presses. And, you cannot query a large press. You must land an agent, who will then shop your manuscript with big-house acquisitions editors on your behalf. It's wickedly hard to get a large-press contract. However, it's relatively easy—if the writing is strong—to land a small-press contract without an agent. The trade-off is that small presses lack meaningful sales networks. Your book will likely not see any bricks-and-mortar placement, and thus not many sales. So it's easier to get published by small presses, with the caveat that you're not likely to make much—if any—money on the deal. In addition, small presses break into "small" and "micro" categories. A press that releases fewer than a dozen titles per year is considered a micro press, and for all practical purposes, their distribution reach is no better than that for a self-published author, given that they lack a sales network and the capital to market titles with major corporate book buyers.

Why should I bother with these weird query requirements? Queries are funny things. Some agents and small presses take a *lassiez-faire* attitude about them; as long as you're in the right ballpark, they'll work with you. Others view the querying process strictly. Fail to jump through every tiny hoop, and you're disqualified before your material even appears before an editor's eyes. As a rule, you should conform precisely to each market's specific query framework. If that framework proves too much bother, then don't pitch that market. Complex query processes serve as something as a friction filter because "lazy" writers won't bother to submit, thus reducing the size of the slush pile. Because those markets tend to receive a smaller number of queries, they might work to your advantage if you've developed genuinely good material to share.

Is there an industry blacklist? Some authors think that their lack of success in landing a query relates to some secret author blacklist maintained by publishing executives. No such list exists. As a publisher, I maintained memberships in several different trade organizations. Only once did I see a specific author named on a general "be on the lookout" email—and he was so flagged only because he had threatened several female editors at several different publications with sexual assault if they rejected his stories. So apart from presenting as a potential serial rapist, odds are good that your failure to find meaningful traction in the open market is not the result of a secret conspiracy against you.

Do I have to give up my rights to get published? No. Authors never assign, transfer, sell, or otherwise relinquish their intellectual property investment in the books they write. Authors *do*, however, license publishers to print, distribute, market, and sell the author's IP investment. Books like novels that follow standard contracts are always issued in the copyright of the author.

Will someone steal my manuscript idea? No. Many authors think that publishers lie in wait, sifting through the slush pile waiting for a good idea they can seize for themselves. Never happens. Almost nothing is original these days.

How long does it take to get published? With a traditional press, assume three years from acceptance to book release. Very tiny, niche presses often move faster, especially for projects like literary journals or anthologies where there's no baked-in process of back-and-forth editing between writers and editors. When you factor edit time, development time, the overhead from other projects, and the tendency for publishers to release once or twice per year, a three-year window is not ideal but also not terrible. Two years are better and more characteristic of high-performing presses. One year is almost unheard-of except for exceptional circumstances.[9]

9: Caffeinted Press's turnaround time for book-length projects ranged from 45 days to three years, with two years serving as a rough average.

Can I use the cool artwork my friend designed for my book cover? Perhaps, if you self-publish, but even then, you'll need a contract with your friend granting you permission to use the artwork commercially. Traditional publishers—with the exception of a few very tiny presses—design covers according to house style conventions. Assume that working with any traditional publisher means you'll forego decision-making authority over covers, fonts, book size, interior arrangement, and front- and back-matter contents. Many small presses nevertheless allow authors to either approve or even to contribute to those elements—but if you assume you can't, yet a publisher invites you in, it's a bonus.

Preparing to Write

Get Fit to Print | 3

You need not be published to be a writer, but if you seek publication, then charting your first steps by means of a deliberate process that incorporates all the tools in the writers' toolkit is better than pouring your heart and soul into a novel right out of the gate—then bewailing that the market determines that this debut novel isn't ready for prime time. In this chapter, we start with a reflection about being too hasty, followed by a 12-month model program that starts at zero and ends with a few short-and-polished pieces ready to send to editors.

3.1 A Marathon, Not a Sprint

Some authors labor under the curious belief that the point of writing is to be published. It isn't.

The point of writing is to write.

Roughly 99.99 percent of all first-time novelists discover no viable traditional market for their manuscript. None. And there's a good reason for it: Writing is hard. Yet publishing is the only industry where new people routinely expect to hit a series-winning grand slam at their very first at-bat. And they do so while holding two contradictory mindsets. First, that "anyone can write," and second, that what *they* wrote is, *ipso facto*, head and shoulders above the crowd.

It's curious that writers are so quick to revel in the complexity of their craft yet equally quick to dismiss the implications of this complexity!

To aspiring authors with ants in their pants over their first manuscript, I say: Don't hurry to publish! In fact, there's no shame in never seeking publication, and much virtue in spending time at the batting cages (we call that time *drafting practice novels*) before you ever approach the plate professionally.

Yes, a full 50 percent of all writers enjoy above-average talent, and 2.5 percent enjoy talent two standard deviations above the mean—whatever that statistic implies. Yes, sometimes, lightning strikes and someone somewhere pens a debut blockbuster novel. But even for that electrified few, think about what they wrote. Most editors aren't of the opinion that stories like *Harry Potter and the Sorcerer's Stone* or *Fifty Shades of Grey* demonstrate breathtaking literary beauty. They met a market need, and that need outweighed the banality of the prose. Yet look at J.K. Rowling now. Her craft—and her Twitter-fu—advanced immeasurably over the years. What might the Harry Potter series have looked like if she had written a half-dozen novels, stashed in a file cabinet somewhere, before she began that charming series that brought her so much acclaim? And for that sliver of authors whose virtue lay in their craft and not in their estimated market appeal—well, you never hear of them, because they usually write lit fic and poetry with academic presses and struggle to move 250 copies of their book over its lifetime.

The biggest mistake emerging writers make consists in shopping the very first manuscript they complete.

The sweet Siren's song enchanting so many into this error isn't easy to resist, for three reasons. First, most people actually writing novels these days aren't coming from a space of deep academic preparation. Small-press leaders only rarely encounter submitters with, say, an MFA or even a bachelor's in creative writing. Instead, the emerging-author profile cuts across all demographics and skill levels. Which is good! But it means that the small tail of genuine, honed talent swims in the same stream as the school of novices who shoal where angels fear to skinny dip. Which is not so good. In such an environment, a statistically average writer still isn't within a country mile of being close enough to warrant a meaningful commercial writing contract. Without a frame of reference for what constitutes *average* and the standard deviations therefrom, people remain blind to their relative strengths and weaknesses.

Second, people bitten by the urge to write tend to write the thing that they really want to write. Sounds eminently circular, doesn't it? The idea that "I've got fire in the belly to write novel X, so I should write novels A, B, C, D, and E first to hone my craft" isn't exactly intuitive. Yet most veteran (published!) writers own a filing cabinet that contains four, five, six, seven different manuscripts. Usually, their first four, five, six, or seven projects. They were labors of love, assuredly, but more importantly, they were *training manuscripts*. They were dress rehearsals to prepare for that first book that really is a viable candidate for publication.

Third, emerging authors invest, psychologically, much more significance into the act of publication than they ought. This misfire sources from two lightly overlapping desires. On one hand, people who sacrifice time and talent over a period of months or years on a manuscript naturally want something to show for it—even if just to justify the effort to long-suffering friends and family—and publication superficially appears to legitimize that investment. On the other hand, writers without a well-functioning and highly competent peer-critique group look to publication as something of an external arbiter of the question, "Am I any good at this whole writing thing?"

Very many writers who've advanced to the "I'm almost done with a book" or "I have a manuscript now" phase of the creative process do not react well to advice about setting aside their first few projects. People get bit by the writing bug and start crafting their dream, thinking that the dream culminates with a book tour starting in Manhattan.[1]

1: I may, early on, have succumbed to Jessica Fletcher Syndrome myself.

Yet a dose of humility and a focus on the discipline of the craft prove the wiser path. In fact, a person who aspires to write a novel ought to get started by *not writing a novel.*

A process that introduces a writer to the essential authors' tools—craft, short fiction, critique groups, peer networks—over a period of time, with opportunity to explore each tool, will better prepare him or her for the long haul than just bellying up to Microsoft Word with no prep, no platform, no expertise, and no sense of the futility they're about to engender.

3.2 A 12-Month Program

Most how-to-be-an-author guides presuppose that you're writing, or have written, material intended for publication. Some writers, however, compartmentalize their writing into public and private spheres. They look at the public writing—the stuff intended for community consumption—as being categorically different from free creative writing, and as their social anxiety peaks, some of them struggle getting started as a "professional" writer.[2]

2: By *professional*, I mean something like *a writer whose work obtains engagement by others through public sharing of that content within the literary marketplace or by means of a writing blog*.

Part of this anxiety hails from a curious and unfortunate tendency among self-proclaimed writing experts to assume that everyone intends to write primarily for publication straight from Day One. As such, Day One assumes a metaphysical significance that, for some emerging writers, prompts existential angst.

Remember: There's no hurry to write for publication, if indeed you ever try! Look at writing as a process—one that you begin deliberately and with just enough structure to keep you moving in the right direction, but without so much artifice that the whole process feels like a series of pointless make-work tasks imposed by a creative-writing professor who's just phoning it in.

One approach to writing mimics a couch-to-5K program: Start small, rehearse the basics, and work your way to more complicated material. This chapter therefore offers a 12-month guide to transitioning from zero to literary hero. Of course, no guided program guarantees that you'll improve your writing or land a publishing contract. But proceeding deliberately will probably lead to fewer self-inflicted injuries than barging ahead blindly—in other words, it'll offer a stronger foundation for your journey from a Zero Percenter to a Ten Percenter.[3]

3: Before you begin, explore whether your family will support the non-trivial time and focus you'll need to write. I've met several writers who roared out of the gate then vanished. And when I'd next see them, they'd say—sometimes in sorrow, sometimes in anger—that their significant other resented the dedicated writing time. So they stopped writing. It's heartbreaking, but situations like this happen frequently.

The Framework

Seven ground rules shape my approach to launching a literary career:

- *Fine-tune your skillset*. Prioritize plugging the gaps in the quality of your construction and your conformance to a recognized style manual, so you don't calcify bad tendencies that will hobble you later. The advice to "just write every day" does you no good, and can actually prove harmful, if you merely reinforce patterns of suboptimal styling. Remember: Practice makes perfect but mindless repetition merely polishes the turd.
- *Quality, not quantity*. Don't stress about "writing every day." Write when you can and don't condemn yourself as a failure if you miss a day or two . . . hundred. Every hour of writing is one hour you didn't previously incur, whether you plan for it daily or accept bits of grace intermittently through the week. Although you should prioritize your writing if you're serious about it, obsessing about times and calendars emphasizes the wrong goal. Your objective isn't to bang a keyboard for X number of hours per day. Rather, focus on cultivating meaningful stories and poems. The quality of the session, and not your words-per-hour, is what matters.

- *Join a tribe.* Find a critique group and make heavy use of it. You will not thrive as a writer in the open market if you think you're an island onto yourself. Editors have a term for self-edited manuscripts—we call them *rejections*, and they're way more obvious to us than they are to the authors who submit them.
- *Build alliances.* Develop relationships with your peers in your local literary scene. You do want someone other than your Great Aunt Ethel to come to your launch party, right? You do want to cultivate relationships with people who can introduce you to professionals who bring you to the next level of literary exposure, right? You can't succeed by sitting, alone, in a café or in your basement writing cave. Writing may be a solitary endeavor, but being a published author takes a network.
- *Platform!* Build a platform and publicly identity as an author—establish a blog, social media, custom domain name, biz cards, etc. Agents and publishers weigh the contribution of your established fan base as part of the profit-and-loss statement that shapes a go/no-go decision for a contract. Although every oppositional-defiant writer who hates social media can point to a few authors who succeeded without a platform, in general, an author who can bring some number of high-confidence sales to the first-quarter performance of a book presents a much smaller risk to publishers than authors who can't.
- *Don't aim too high, too fast.* Start small, with short stories and poems, as a gateway to novel writing. The least successful writers tend to be folks who've never written for publication, then they pen their debut novel, and then they lament that no one pays attention to their manuscript. Before you write a novel, write short stories. Write poems. Workshop them. Present them to literary journals and magazines and anthologies. Figure out how to write in short, digestible chunks before you invest years of your life scribbling a book that no one but Great Aunt Ethel pretends to like. Plus, earning writing credits in the short-form market bolsters your credibility with agents and editors when you finally write a novel worth publishing.
- *Play the long game.* Assume that the first five long-form books you write will never be shopped to an agent or an editor, and that each of your books—including the training manuscripts—will take you between one and two years to complete.[4] Got a brilliant idea for the story that's been burning in your chest since you were a teenager? Great. Write five other novels first. By then, your craft will have advanced to the point that you're free to develop your passion project without dooming it by imprudent haste.

4: Some writers churn out two manuscripts per year; some authors churn out one every two years. I've worked with several authors who each spent more than eight years writing a single novel.

Month by Month

If you internalize these seven points, you're in good shape. Miss any of them, and you'll pay the price later. To help you advance in light of these points, consider the following 12-month program.

January: Grok Your Toolkit January doesn't include any writing, just studying. You'll arm yourself with the essential reference manuals of a

Month	Goal
January	Build your toolkit
February	Three (short) first drafts
March	Revisions; peer networking
April	Join a tribe; set your writing environment
May	Launch your platform
June	Reinforce your first drafts
July	Write a novelette
August	Network more, network harder
September	Self-editing
October	Novel-length planning
November	Novel-length zero drafting
December	Shopping short fiction

Table 3.1: Summary of Major Monthly Activities

writer, then explore them in enough detail to understand what's in them. Your goal isn't to *read* these books, except perhaps the memoirs. Instead, you should become familiar with their content and structure to develop insight about when you should refer to them while you write.[5]

5: Chapter 6 addresses these recommended texts.

Also, scope out your local literary scene. Check Facebook, Eventbrite, local writing groups, your library system, local colleges—try to figure out what literary events occur and on what frequency. Pay particular attention to venues for readings and open-access writers' groups because both will surface later in the year. Your friendly neighborhood librarians are well-positioned to help you with this research.

Consider, too, taking online courses in grammar and syntax to sharpen your saw. EdX offers a free "English Grammar and Style" class; Coursera offers a Creative Writing concentration, with a mix of free and paid classes; Stanford University offers a paid Creative Writing online program. Or look for local options, including through your local library system or community college.

Some creative-writing training is good but sometimes you'll encounter too much of a good thing. Modern creative-writing programs tend to fetishize "craft" and workshopping and the exploration of sociopolitical themes. And in moderation, these attributes are surely salutary. But experienced editors spot capital-W *workshopped* material from a mile away—this stuff tends to be a bit too precious, a bit too on-the-nose woke, a bit too abstract, a bit too free-verse, a bit too solipsistic. Proceed with caution.[6]

6: When you encounter a person who lists as core influences a litany of people you've never heard of, and when you search for those influences you wonder how anyone could have heard of them, odds are good you're working with someone deeply enmeshed in Creative Writing Culture. Your best bet? Walk away slowly, without making eye contact or sudden movements. Try distracting them, if necessary, with an artisanal fountain pen or a tin of beard balm or a Sylvia Plath refrigerator magnet.

Read some acclaimed short fiction and poetry. No better way to learn the craft than by observing its masterworks. Look for resources like *The Best American Short Stories* or the annual Pushcart Prize volume. Collections that span longer periods of time prove interesting, too; the best stuff from, say, 1915 doesn't look anything like stories and poems from 2015. You'd be well served, however, by avoiding content that focuses on material after 1990. Not only is it "too new" and thus suffers from immediacy bias, but many contemporary editors now superimpose highly precise themes that often distract from a broader view of the craft. These themes aren't inherently problematic, but they offer a heavier curator's touch compared to editors from yesteryear.

January will seem like a dry exercise, but reading stylebooks is like looking at maps: Not fun, but unless you do it, you don't know what you don't know about getting from Point A to Point B.

So your goal this month is to spend a minimum of 20 hours studying these reference volumes in detail. That's it. No writing. Just studying. And if you elect to read acclaimed short fiction or memoirs, that time serves in addition to the 20 hours you spend exploring your new reference collection.

February: First Drafts The shortest month demands the most painful trudge before the keyboard. Write one of each of the following: a poem of at least 20 lines, a flash story between 500 and 1,000 words, a creative non-fiction essay between 1,000 and 2,500 words, and a short story between 2,500 and 5,000 words. Write them in this order.

Start on 2/1 and be done by 2/28. One item per week.

These pieces will likely be rough around the edges. That's okay. The point is to do the writing. You'll use this content later to hone your self-edit chops and to develop material for workshopping with a critique group. Before then, however, you must commit something to paper. You'll also learn while you work a bit about how you write: Morning or evening? PC or paper? Notes first or dive "write" in then revise later? Don't overthink it. Let it feel natural. There's no objectively correct way to proceed.[7]

7: Although *The Diction Dude Guide to the Mechanics of Fiction* addresses questions of structure and syntax, I've assembled 50 "informed suggestions" that are a bit craft-heavy to help get you started. See Chapter 7 for the list.

The only rules this month are to write the words. You're free to pick your genres, poem styles, themes, subjects, and whatnot. Don't self-edit. *Just write.*

And don't stress about the poem, either. The point of poetry for fiction writers is to focus on the interplay of form, diction, and rhythm. You cannot be a sublime craftsperson of fiction if you can't at least try to write poor-to-middlin' cat poetry.[8] A novelist who writes bad poetry is still (usually) a better novelist than the person who can't be bothered to experiment in verse every now and then.

8: As I do.

"But, but, but—it's gonna be awful!" you lament.

Yup. That's the point.

The stuff you write in February will recur throughout the year. You'll self-edit it and you'll cycle through it with a peer critique group. But you can't do any of those things until you've generated an ink-upon-paper artifact.

This part of the process—the drafting part—is where a goodly number of writers sashay away from the table. For aspiring writers, the act of creating a first real story or poem is just as significant to them, psychologically, as birthing a child. And this significance sometimes erects psychological roadblocks manifested as procrastination, self-doubt, and anxiety.

Here's the thing: When you birth your first word-babies, they're going to be young. Raw. You'll look at them and you'll likely cry. Strangers who catch a whiff of them suspect that a diaper needs changing. *All that is normal.* Don't let the fear of creating something imperfect stop you from creating anything at all! Trust the Diction Dude when he tells you that all the anxiety, strong as it may be, is a necessary prelude to delivering meaningful art. So, yes. Your word-baby won't be perfect. But you know what? *You made something*. Fine-tuning it—like potty-training a toddler—takes much patience and persistence. You'll get there. For now, pour your heart upon Microsoft Word without mental reservation or purpose of evasion. You'll have some setbacks, but in the end, you and your work product will be far better because your courage to create trumped your penchant to procrastinate.

March: Revise and Network Attend at least one literary event in your community—a book signing, a poetry reading, whatever. Better yet, attend more than one. And when you're there, socialize with people.[9]

9: If your community is locked down thanks to Covid-19, get creative—but don't skip the networking component altogether.

Start to build connections with your local literary community. You need a network of fellow literary travelers if you want to be successful as a published writer—so socialize with fellow authors, readers, publishers, editors, booksellers, etc. This networking component is a major contributor to the financial viability of first-time authors.

You will not succeed as an author if you eschew human contact. It's true that when you write, you write alone. But it's not true that you can succeed as a commercially viable author solely on your merits. To thrive, you must nurture a network of peers whom you support and vice-versa. The higher up the literary food chain you go, the more significance accrues to your alma mater or to your network. The reason that so many Iowa grads find it easy to place content in highfalutin literary journals isn't necessarily because these writers are *good*, but because they're networked.[10] The network effect governs all industries; you're mistaken if you think publishing is any different.

10: Of course, many of them are fantastic. But being fantastic plus being networked? Even better.

So find a mentor and an advocate. Connect to peers. Survey the relationship map of your local literary community and do your best to slide into it. Go with a friend if you're naturally shy.

Also, revise your February pieces. Don't stress about the right way to edit. Just do what comes naturally. And don't show them to anyone else yet. Not even Great Aunt Ethel.

April: Join a Tribe and Lock a Protocol Find or join a critique group. Aim for a group that's open, focused, and diverse in terms of experience. Think about the folks you met in March. For without beta readers—a trusted critique group—your path to success becomes significantly steeper.

When you're in a group, you'll be expected to submit stuff for review.[11] The results will probably be painful. And you'll be expected to reciprocate. That process will likely prove painful, too. But it's the best and most accessible infrastructure at your disposal for improving your writing.

11: See Chapter 5 for more information about writers' groups.

Also this month: Settle on your toolset—times, tools, and rituals. You won't be bound to it forever, but you'll commit to it for the rest of this program. Selecting a writing environment now stops you from spending so much time planning to write, and continuously tweaking that environment, that you never get around to *actually* writing. So you'll have to stick with your choice, knowing that the lessons you learn about what works and what doesn't can be incorporated in Month 13.

Some people enjoy sitting at the kitchen counter with a laptop and Microsoft Word. Others prefer planning in OneNote and drafting in Scrivener. Still others favor plain-text Markdown or AsciiDoc or $\LaTeX$. And while some folks love early-morning scribbling, others need the evening and a martini to stimulate the creative juices. Or a jaunt to the coffee shop. Or a Holy Hour at the local Catholic church. Or a walk in the county park. Regardless, prepare your planned times for writing with the tools you find most useful. Make this combination of tools, time, and setting a habit.

May: Platform Start building a business and social platform.

Now's the time to "come out" as a writer. Build a blog. Establish a Twitter account and a Facebook fan page for yourself as an author. Create a Goodreads author account. Think about your author's identity: Do you use a pseudonym? Set up a different email address or a PO Box for your literary endeavors? Do you establish an LLC or a DBA to legally and financially separate your author-related work from your personal life? Do you need your own logo or Web domain? Author-branded business cards?[12]

12: See the last chapter for more context.

Collect ideas about other short stories or poems you could write, but take this month to address your professional infrastructure.

Don't, by the way, diminish the value of maintaining a writers' blog. Emerging writer pooh-pooh it, because it "takes time away from writing." Yet a blog also helps you to write, plus it connects you with future readers. And if you incorporate a sign-up form for your email newsletter—which you should!—then you're on your way to developing a meaningful author platform, provided you actually send newsletters.[13]

13: Snag a copy of *The Diction Dude Essential Guide to Growing a Platform* for a book-length treatment on this subject. When it's released, that is.

June: Reinforcement Edit your February works in light of feedback from your critique group.

You'll probably be embarrassed by what your critique partners catch. Good. Learn from the experience. And if you disagree with their observations, don't just dismiss the comments—study them. You have to grow a certain amount of skin thickness as a writer and lose a degree of emotional attachment to your work to survive in a tough literary market. Some people can't handle feedback well. If you're one of those folks, re-consider your aspiration to write for publication. Writers closed to feedback struggle even harder to succeed.

Build your social platform by blogging at least once per week and growing your Facebook likes and Twitter followers. Aim for slow, organic growth. Keep performing this network-acquisition work, from now until the day you die. Social media is a long-term endeavor. It'll likely be years before you grow a substantial following. Stick with it. Your time investment today will eventually pay off, despite the painfully slow progress you'll make over the first year or five.

July: More Writing Write a novelette. Longer-form works (aim for 14k to 16k words) require more complex plotting, character development, and narrative arcs. You'll build on the lessons you learned with shorter works, earlier in the year, to voyage into more complicated waters.

Novelettes are funny beasts: They're longer than short stories but not as long as novellas. They're difficult to place for publication. They're long enough that you really do need to plan them and make full use of your characterization and conflict tools, but they're not so long that the plot can become too complex. It's a hard length to write but a good length to learn to write.

August: More Networking Attend one writing-related event each week. Don't write much. Instead, read the stuff your local peers have published. Your talent as a writer must be honed, in part, by being a voracious reader. Writers who don't read are like electricians living in a candle-lit house, who scribble with a dull pencil incoherent similes upon the walls. Don't be that guy. He's creepy.

Continue to build your network. Pass out your business cards, buy local authors' books, show up at readings. Meet people. Learn from their stories and purchase their books. Get to know the names of well-known local writers and artists. One day, when you need a quote for a book cover, these are the folks to whom you'll turn. And when you throw your book-launch party, these are the people who will show up to celebrate with you.

September: More Reinforcement Edit your novelette in light of feedback from your critique group.

Learn from critique feedback. Assess where you have gaps (descriptions, point of view, narrative voice, setting, conflict, etc.) and go back to your reference materials to study appropriate solutions.

Keep growing your social network.

October: Plotting at Length Plan a novel. Target 85,000 words for the completed product. Do not start writing it yet, but do think about plot, characters, conflict, setting, etc.[14]

14: The next chapter addresses book planning at a high level.

Long-form plotting without writing makes you think about what you're doing before you do it. You might enjoy "pantsing" (writing without prep), but you should at least once try the discipline of planning.

Also, write two short stories of fewer than 5,000 words each. Even when you're in plotting/revising modes, still find the time to write short pieces. Build your own slush pile. It'll come in handy when you come across a great submission opportunity on deadline day!

November: NaNoWriMo Participate in National Novel Writing Month. Your goal is to start on November 1 and by November 30, be "done" with a manuscript of at least 50k words. (The novel need not be complete, you just need to have incurred 50,000 validated words by 11:59 p.m. on the 30th.)

This novel is considered a *zero draft*—it's not even a first draft. That's OK. Don't spend time self-editing as you go. And don't aim to write a 50,000-word story; most first-time novels are closer to 80,000 to 90,000 words long. Your goal is to just get the first 50,000 words down. You'll expand the story and fix your zero draft later.

December: Submissions Pick at least two of your completed, peer-reviewed short-form pieces. Send each to at least a dozen contests, anthologies or literary journals. Check *Poets & Writers* or the annual *Writer's Market* for an excellent, current list of opportunities. You are likely to get a lot of silence, or a lot of form rejections—but we all do. Keep writing, keep submitting. Learn from your feedback and from your ongoing study of good stories and reference materials.

Fine-tune your October stories in light of feedback from your critique group.

Finish your November novel.[15] It's probably going to be garbage, and that's good, because it's a starting point for the editing and redrafting process—it'll help you figure out the things you didn't realize you needed to work on. Your next two or three novels are likely to also be weak. Embrace the suck; it makes you stronger.

15: If you can. Writing a standard-length novel for the first time in two months is a huge lift; it's not unusual for people to spend years working at it. But remember, this process is a training manuscript culminating in a zero draft. Perfection here is the enemy of progress.

3.3 Happily Ever After?

So what happens in Month 13? Basically: Rinse and repeat, then read Chapter 8 of this book.

There's no guaranteed pathway to publication. None whatsoever. If you fine-tune your skills, focus on the quality of your writing rather than the amount of time you spend behind the keyboard, join a tribe, build alliances, develop your platform, start small and aim low, and play the long game—well, these habits insulate you from the path of so many disillusioned novelists who type the Great American Novel with no writing history, no platform, no critique group to offer feedback, no peers to serve as referral partners, and no sense of how the calendar and the industry work.

Success in publishing follows from two pathways. The first—the Path of Serendipity—hopes you'll catch lightning in a bottle. You likely won't, unless you've bribed the Goddess of Luck by interning at a high-circulation literary journal or matriculating from a prestigious MFA program. Luck favors the connected; connection sometimes trumps talent.

The second route—the Path of Labor—starts from zero but bootstraps into something bigger than zero. The Get Fit to Print idea assumes you'll trudge the Path of Labor. There's still plenty of opportunity for Lady Luck to smile upon you or to pull the rug out from beneath you. But the best you can do is to prepare as thoroughly you can, secure in the knowledge that most authors don't.

A Cadence Each writer proceeds at his or her own pace. There's no "right" number of stories to craft in a defined period of time, no "right" amount of time to craft a novel. But if you work through the Get Fit to Print program, you'll start to figure out how long it takes you to generate a solid first draft of a given unit of story. From there, you're free to plan your writing future.

A word of advice, though—the more you vary lengths, genres, and formats, the more you'll stretch your ability. Even if you aspire to become the next great sci-fi novelist, write short stories. Pen the occasional poem. You'll be well-served to maintain a slush pile of at least a dozen or so short stories, or two dozen poems, or a handful of personal essays, that you're free to shop on deadline to various journals or awards programs.

Never stop writing. And never start writing the same darn thing, over and over again.

Book Planning | 4

Writing for yourself is perfectly legitimate, but if you intend to write for publication, you must master the craft as editors expect to see it. In this chapter, after a reflection about preparing to write, we'll explore the thorny question of what *to write, followed by standards for manuscript formatting.*

4.1 Planning a Book

In the universe of writers, two camps battle for literary supremacy: The Planners, who've never met an outline they couldn't augment, and the Pantsers, who've never met an outline they couldn't disregard.

Despite the myriad blog posts and books that promise a surefire planning approach to help you achieve your wildest writing dreams, there's no super-ultra-elite magic crafting technique or software suite guaranteed to deliver results. No system that helps you write more effectively that you can simply adopt as your own.

Gamblers invest time and money in various betting systems—the Martingale, the Modified Martingale, Fibonacci, Oscar's Grind, Cancellation—that, statistically, are no better (and sometimes worse!) than random chance alone. Some writers think similarly: If only Fortuna blessed them with the right computer program or mechanical keyboard or writing space or notebook system or storycrafting technique, all the writers' block would vanish and Nobel-contending literature would gush forth. Rarely do these aspiring scribes consider the degree to which obsessing about their writing process distracts them from actually writing.

Your methods of preparation and of committing words to paper are unique to you. No other authors follow your approach or, conversely, magically empower you with their own secret sauce. Although there's surely some ancillary benefit to seeing how others structure their craft, we examine our peers' approaches with an eye toward tips-and-tricks appropriation and fine-tuning, not wholesale mimicry.

My own experiences as a novelist testify to this truth.

My very first, unsuccessful, attempt at writing long-form fiction followed the conventional approach to Pantsing. A friend of mine—an experienced self-published novelist named Duane—suggested that I join him for this thing called "National Novel Writing Month." To that point, I was almost exclusively an essayist, having worked my way up from opinion columnist to opinion editor to editor in chief of a small daily newspaper. I could place 800 mostly flawless words of a staff editorial on the page in 15 minutes flat. I had to, every damned day.

So a novel? Of 50,000 words developed over 30 full days? How hard could *that* be?

Duane invited me to participate on October 30. On the first of November, NaNoWriMo started, and I was both shocked and amused to discover myself surrounded by a great unwashed herd of enthusiasts—armed with laptops, notepads, and even typewriters—banging out attempts at fantasy and romance and sci-fi. I figured I'd sit down, write the book, call it a win, and move on with my life. So I started drafting a detective story in true Pantser style: No prep work, just Microsoft Word and the choice of a genre. I wrote the first chapter, which started with a murder in a crowded theater, and then I realized I didn't know who died, or why, or even who did it and why the death mattered.

I failed miserably even as fellow herd members notched end-of-month wins. *Books are hard.*

The next year, I resolved to do better. I tried my hand at sci-fi, so never having written a novel before, I boldly penned a one-page summary for a trilogy and planned to use that NaNoWriMo to write Book One. I got farther this time but I still crashed and burned. At one point, for example, I lost three full days working through the physics and biomechanics of a grain of sand hitting a spacewalking astronaut at 40 percent of the speed of light.[1]

1: Turns out, you don't want that scenario to happen to you. It also turns out that hyper-precision about the math related to an irrelevant factoid isn't a virtue during the zero-draft phase.

NaNoWriMo eventually became a matter of pride: If I could write researched, reasoned, page-ready editorials in my sleep, why couldn't I just *make stuff up?*

For my third foray into November shenanigans, I adjusted yet again: I planned, in excruciating detail, on a scene-by-scene level. And you know what? This time it mostly worked. My core insight was that I couldn't craft a plot on the fly. I needed it planned in advance and chunked into chapters and scenes; with that scaffolding in place, writing became an exercise in meeting a defined content goal, rather than an exercise of planning-while-writing.

Then again, some folks in my writing group perform no meaningful planning at all yet still manage to turn out stories that show real promise. Different strokes for different folks. So let me share my own approach—which you're free to study but not to photocopy.

Important!

The steps outlined below represent one writer's approach to novel planning. These steps work for me; I don't pretend that they represent a best practice that most other writers ought to emulate. The examples in the figures are deliberately first-draft rough and inconsistent, too. As should yours be when you begin your own planning process! They'll firm up as your work unfolds.

The Diction Dude's Noveling Method in "Eight" "Easy" "Steps" Behold, the process undergirding my literary workflow.

1. *Cultivate the merest whisper of an idea.* I don't plan a story concept, but rather I record attributes I wish to include in "a" story. This process usually takes about three or four months, and I'll end up with a list in Microsoft OneNote of a few dozen topics that keep

bubbling up during conversations, daydreams, showers, or nature walks. For one novel, the list included such attributes as:

- teen murdered by same-sex lover
- sympathetic Catholic priest
- set in rural Michigan
- secret archive
- powerful family with long-suppressed secret
- tattoo of a phoenix
- protagonist deals with broken relationship
- horse farms

Usually, a thematic concept bubbles up through these varied signals. It's not unusual for me to develop several separate ticker lists, some of which I act upon and others that I archive if they don't cohere.

2. *Use a whiteboard to craft a crude network diagram of people who will appear in this story*. That process starts blindly; I don't already know who the people are. Rather, I just start drawing circles, one per character, then I connect them. Then I give the circles roles, then names. This initial process is mostly random—how many circles and lines? I don't know until I stop making them. Then I redraw the connections as roles firm up, and along those spokes I indicate the nature of the relationship, until there's a dotted web (a *network diagram*) on the whiteboard.[2] Importantly, this web in its final form represents the state of the universe on the day before Page 1 begins: Mapping roles and relationships among named characters is generally all the "backstory" I require, and it has the benefit of not being especially amenable to a Chapter 1 data dump. It also, I think, ensures that the cast of characters enjoys relationships beyond what's necessary to advance a linear plot. Makes for richer storytelling, I think. *See Figure 4.1.*

2: Using a drawing tool with your tablet-and-stylus setup works, too.

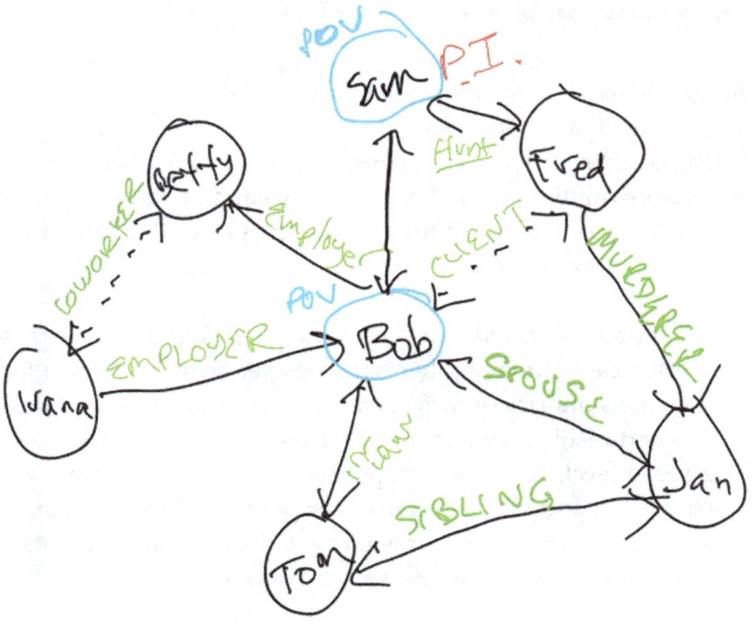

Figure 4.1: A basic character-relationship (network) diagram.

3. *Identify the main character from within the relationship web and then, in light of the relationship web and the attributes list, determine the core conflict of the story*. I'll then select a suitable number of characters

who earn point-of-view privileges within the story. This character list includes primary, secondary, and placeholder people—sketched, at the outset, in terms of archetypes. And the core conflict, informed in part by the relationship web and in part by the attributes list, coheres to archetypes, too. Archetypical roles, plots, and conflicts are your friend; the more you deviate from them, the more your story diverges from the genre norms that editors and agents honor as signs of market viability.

4. *Use the conflict, the relationship web, and the attributes list to draft a brief story concept.* Develop a specific genre and word-count target for the project. Here, I also refine the thematic statement. I'm not yet focused on plot points, but rather on the foundation—genre, conflict, archetype. Limit the story concept to no more than 250 words. *See Figure 4.2.*

GENRE & WORD COUNT: Hardboiled detective (65k words).

CONFLICTS: Bob's anguish over his final conversation with Jan before her murder; Sam's search for the murderer to restore her self-confidence; Fred's desire for revenge on an old perceived injury.

STORY CONCEPT:

- Bob, an investment banker with a good life, argues with his wife the night before the story begins. On his way to the office the next morning, he's called by the police. His wife Jan had been murdered. He is anguished. The police have no leads, so he hires Sam, a cynical private investigator who's haunted by her inability to solve a prior case. While Sam searches for clues and struggles with imposter syndrome, Bob works through his shame over his last conversation with Jan, including an angry outburst at her funeral and conversations with his brother-in-law and his boss. Meanwhile, Sam finds two major clues that lead him to Fred, a client of Bob's who was angry that Bob's portfolio strategy wiped him out. Sam finds hard evidence and arranges with the police to have Fred arrested. The arrest brings closure for Bob, who begins to heal the relationships he damaged over the years, as well as Sam, whose self-confidence is restored.

THEMATIC STATEMENT: The value of relationships lies not in any one moment of weakness and failure but in the way we relate over the long haul.

Figure 4.2: An example of a brief story concept.

5. *Expand the story concept—again, using a whiteboard—into a three-act story structure complete with inflection points for rising and falling action that correspond to chapters.* Specific plot sequences are governed by the core conflict; plot and conflict work hand-in-hand.[3] This is the point where I outline both the main plot as well as one or more subplots. *See Figure 4.3.*

3: In fact, when I draft the plot arc, I include the conflict arc in a different ink color, correlating conflict touchpoints with plot inflections.

6. *Identify the touchpoints that must be addressed in each chapter to make it work.* Determine number of scenes per chapter. Write a three-sentence summary of each scene and stipulate a target word count. The end result is an annotated table of contents for the book, to a scene level, with each chapter or scene marked with a word-count goal and identification of the point-of-view character. The summary references not only plot activity but conflict points that must initiate, persist or resolve. *See Figure 4.4.*

7. *Draft brief sketches of people and places and log them in my project-notes file.* I try to fully understand the characters and settings before I write, because "discovering" them as I write usually means that everything I wrote before the fullness of discovery must

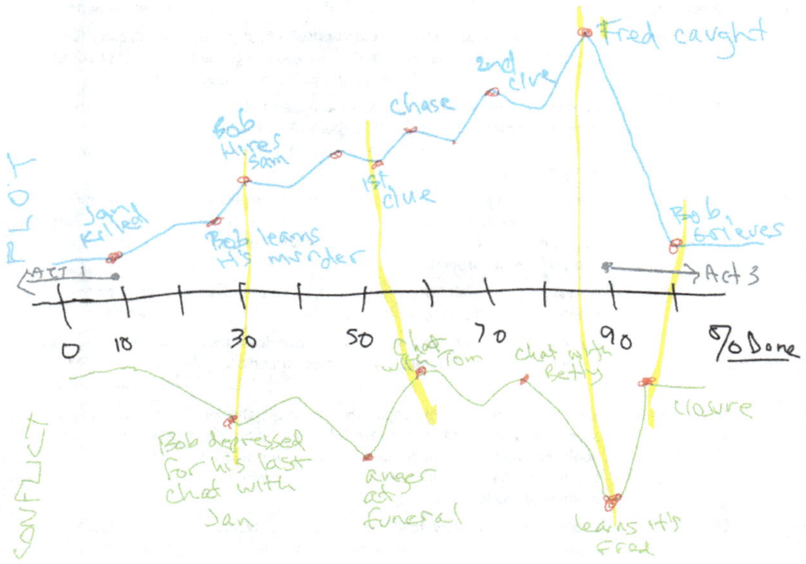

Figure 4.3: A working model for a plot-conflict outline.

be rewritten. It also slows my roll if I have to invent a person or place as I'm writing. Plus, these kinds of place-and-people vignettes make for great blog-post fodder to keep your audience engaged while squelching the urge to lard backstory into the real manuscript. As a bonus, because I keep a single file with all these sketches, then as something significant happens to a character, or I must insert a fact not previously sketched, I update that file real-time so I avoid continuity errors within the manuscript. Few things are as frustrating during self-edits as coming across a reference to something, like a character's hair color, and develop a sinking feeling that you identified the color differently . . . *somewhere* . . . within the novel.

8. *Write the book.* With the seven planning steps completed, my writing process consists of picking a scene and writing it according to the spec I had already determined. I'm not locked into picking up where I left off; if I'm not happy with Scene X, I can instead pick up Scene Y or Scene Z instead. Because I draft in plain text using LaTeXmarkup and rely upon Microsoft Visual Studio Code as my writing environment, I display a pane for the active chapter; a quarter-sized pane for overall status and project notes; a pane with the technical data for the book and the active bibliography; and an Explorer pane listing project files, chapter outlines, a revision-history timeline, and my list of project to-dos. *See Figure 4.5.*

This approach works well for me—for projects like *The Diction Dude Essential Guides* series as well as for novels and even short fiction and essays. It may or may not work for you.

Regardless of your method, develop a process that *does* work for you. Otherwise, you'll end up Pantsing it. Which, while not intrinsically wrong, will require for most writers a significantly increased time-and-effort commitment, usually in the form of additional rounds of heavy revision, to generate stories well-founded for eventual commercial publication.

Some people thrive on Pantsing; they basically write the story, tweak it a

Ch.	Words	POV	Plot Points	Conflict Points
1	5500	Bob	Bob called by police. Pulls over. Calls Betty, his boss, to say he's not coming into the office. Tells Betty about argument the night before. Goes home to wait for police interview.	Shock and shame at his final words to his wife.
2	5000	Bob	Interview at police station. Bob is not a suspect but detectives probe and he must ID the body. Police have no leads; he gets mad and threatens to hire a PI. The cops shrug him off.	Intense pain at seeing her corpse.
3	6000	Sam	Wakes up with a hangover, trudges into the office. She gets a VM from Bob, who called her based on a referral. She calls him, agrees to take the case. She calls the detective and gets the run-around.	Fear of failing to solve yet another murder.
4	5500	Sam	Attends Jan's funeral. Observes Bob's angry behavior and the dynamics of the people in attendance.	Fear of missing something.
5	5000	Bob	Bob talks to Tom, Jan's brother. Tom talks him down the anger scale a bit, but advises Bob that he's burned a lot of bridges.	Shame deepens as Bob realizes how far he's fallen in recent years.
6	6000	Sam	Sam checks the stories of people whose funeral behavior seemed odd. She narrows in on Fred, who signed the guest book. Fred had a prior arrest for domestic violence. More significantly, he lost a lot of money six months before -- money Bob managed.	Imposter syndrome as she feels she's found something relevant ... again.
7	5500	Bob	Another chat with Betty, followed by a chat with Ivana. Bob discovers that Tom's comment about his abrasive personality hit home.	Disorientation about his collapsing worldview.
8	5000	Sam	Sam visits a friend (a former ex) who manages a telecom store. She sweet-talks her into checking the location pings on Tom's phone. The pings put him going toward and away from the building, with a gap. Sam then visits the security office of Jan's office building. She sees Fred's car on CCTV.	Excitement builds as she makes significant case headway.
9	6000	Sam	Sam meets the detective, who is aware of Fred but lacks probable cause for a warrant. Sam pitches a trap.	More excitement.
10	6000	Bob	Bob meets Sam, who tells him her theory about Fred. He is shocked. To close the case, Bob must confront Fred -- but with the police monitoring in the next room. He agrees.	Righteous indignation boils over.
11	6000	Sam	Sam arranges for Bob to meet with Fred. The two spar verbally. Bob's own anger issues help him coax Fred into an angry outburst where he admits to the murder. The police enter the room.	Sam's earlier self-doubt vanishes.
12	4000	Bob	Bob and Tom have dinner. Bob expresses vulnerability and asks for help in being a better person. Tom agrees to help.	Bob realizes he's been wrong and commits to doing better.

Figure 4.4: A working model for chapter-by-chapter plot-and-conflict story.

bit, realize it's a first draft, then rewrite it *in toto*. And it works! If you've cultivated the discipline to edit heavily and rewrite without mercy, this loosey-goosey voyage of exploration might be your jam. But the more resistant you are to editing and major revision, the more you'll benefit from precise preparation—especially given that the guardrails for what's welcome in the commercial-publication space are narrower than most emerging authors realize.

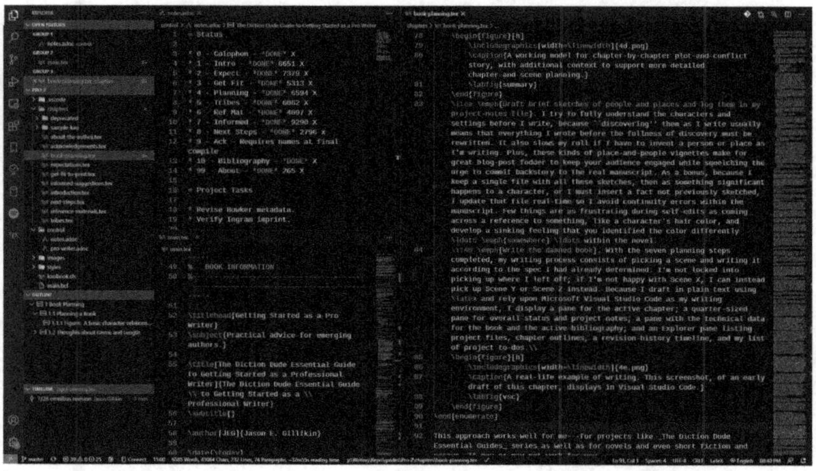

Figure 4.5: A real-life example of writing in progress.

4.2 Genre and Length

A PERSON WRITING FOR FUN need not observe any specific constraints, but a person writing for commercial publication isn't so fortunate. As I often tell authors: *Don't think about what book you want to write; think about what book you want to sell.* Because if you can't sell the book, it'll never grace a bookshelf.

Length

Although there's no such thing as an "average" book, it's generally the case that for most long-form fiction, debut authors' manuscripts ought to clock in somewhere around 85,000 words. Obviously, the rules differ based on genre—an illustrated children's book might be only a few hundred words, for example—but for most novels, aim for 85k.

The tricksy question: How far away from 85k can you stray and still remain market viable?

Different genres admit to different expected lengths. A space opera at 120k might be perfectly fine, whereas a romance novel that long is probably less okay. Word count is more pressing at the lower ends of the scale, however, because a low-count book tends to develop an unfavorable print cost per unit of sale that adversely affects projected profit-and-loss estimates.[4] Most editors are temperamentally more inclined to accept a bit-too-long manuscript with an eye toward trimming it than a bit-too-short manuscript that may require substantial editing to get into a targeted word-count range. So err, if you must, on the side of heft. But not too much heft!

4: Unless you go e-book only.

Adult genre novels Avoid shopping adult genre novels of fewer than 60k words. They're hard to price: A print book entails some degree of fixed costs to develop and produce, but retail consumers tend to shy away from "small" books with normal-to-large price points. If your work is around 45k to 50k and you cannot make it bigger, consider shortening it to turn it into a novella-length piece. Novellas aren't really sold as stand-alone print books anymore, but they'll often do okay e-book only, or as part of a collection of several novellas.

Poetry collections Poetry collections don't admit to hard-and-fast specifics, but from a classification perspective, a book of one or two dozen or so short poems is generally considered a *chapbook*. Beyond that, it's a poetry book, although the larger the book, the tougher it remains to keep a tight discipline about a theme unifying the individual poems.

Non-fiction books Creative non-fiction generally mirrors novels, but with the exception that in some cases, the addition of non-text content like photos and illustrations and works-cited sections adds to the page count without adding to the word count, partially offsetting a smaller manuscript size. Technical non-fiction usually is as long as it needs to be to get the job done. Pricing strategy for non-fiction texts tends to differ based on the target market. A book intended for sale to college bookstores may be priced differently from a book offered by a professional association's online store, versus a price for general retail consumers—a market segment called *adult trade*, and which usually serves as the default segment.

Genre—Non-Fiction

Non-fiction books *can* do well, but it's harder to sell a non-fiction title without a meaningful platform unless you meld into the hazy zone of certain business non-fiction books. A lot of non-fiction books in hyper-niche markets usually follow a self- or vanity-published lifecycle.

There's no formal rule about it, but in general, non-fiction breaks into several categories. Highly technical non-fiction (e.g., computer-programming books) generally receive a treatment quite unlike a novel might.[5] Creative non-fiction—stuff like essays or personal reflections—usually doesn't sell well at book length, which is why much creative non-fiction appears in short form, through literary journals and anthologies. Business non-fiction, which includes material like cookbooks, parenting guides, religious devotionals, politics-and-culture explorations, and the like, are all over the board. In some cases, you need tight credentials and a strong platform; in others, less so.

5: For example, they're rarely written in a word processor. Instead, they are written in a plain-text markup syntax within a publisher-developed template.

It's best to fully dive into the economics and editorial practices of the specific non-fiction world you seek to inhabit, because variation is high and deviation isn't all that welcome.

Genre—Fiction

For genre fiction, manuscript length is only one consideration. The other follows from the 2018 Authors Guild survey, which discovered that median author-related income in 2017 was highest (by a factor of five!) for self-published romance and romantic suspense writers compared to the next-highest tier of mysteries and thrillers.[3]

The market differs, too, between self-published and traditionally published authors. In self-published markets, a focus on romance, sci-fi, and fantasy does well, followed by mystery and crime thrillers. In the traditional market, many of the bestsellers are one-off hits by politicians or genre blockbusters, but from a genre perspective, romance and crime top the list, followed by religious inspiration, followed by sci-fi/fantasy, followed by horror.

Literary fiction is a bust, financially, as are things like memoirs—unless you're famous. And as the Authors Guild survey revealed, mid-list is effectively non-existent.

Different genres support different platform expectations. People who write high-churn/low-loyalty content, like romance e-books, often don't need a platform at all, whereas fantasy and sci-fi writers often thrive because of a built-in audience that follows the author. Literary fiction almost never requires a platform—credentials and prestige publication history matter more than mail-list sizes—but mass-market genre fiction often lives or dies based on mail-list sizes. It's not an accident that a supermarket bookstore's fiction section tends to be dominated by the same few dozen high-profile writers. So trying to shop a major-lift project like a nine-volume epic space-opera magic saga when your platform consists of fewer than 100 active leads is, uh, *bold*.

To Fuse or Not to Fuse?

A *fusion* story blends genres. They can be a ton of fun. They're also, for all practical purposes, unpublishable.

A book that tries to blend fiction and non-fiction, or a book that merges several fiction genres into a single narrative, rarely finds a home. The reason is straightforward: All books in the commercial book market must obtain an International Standard Book Number. The agency that assigns ISBNs in the United States, R.R. Bowker, allows for limited genre-identification of an enrolled title. This limited data pushes to the Books In Print database. The thing is, genres aren't additive. You pick *one* from a very short list. If the book doesn't really fit that genre's norms, then no reputable publisher will touch it, because no bookstore will buy it, because no two bookstore clerks will know which section of the store marks the optimal placement for that book.[6]

6: Distribution catalogs often support several genre flags, but the problem on the bookstore end is still the same: One book belongs on one shelf in one genre-based section.

So your clever story about lesbian aliens solving a mystery and falling in love in Imperial Rome—well, it's a good candidate for self-publishing, or placement with a hyper-niche small press that offers effectively zero distribution reach.

(Which doesn't mean *don't write it*. I only mean that fusion stories, while often delightful, rarely prove commercially viable because of this metadata-and-discovery problem. So if it's publication credits and wide distribution you seek, fuse your genres with an spirit of awe and trembling.)

4.3 Other Considerations

When you write a story intended for publication, your freedom to stray from generally accepted conventions narrows. Some of those conventions reflect emerging literary and economic trends in the industry. Six of these are worth highlighting for emerging authors.

1. *Literary fiction prioritizes elegant writing.* One reason lit-fic is so popular with the Master of Fine Arts crowd relates to its tight correspondence to *program fiction*. Most successful lit-fic published today favors precocious styles featuring lots of rare words, belabored imagery, and highly emotive scenes. It's more of an impressionistic art form—painting the messy human condition with words—than most genre fiction, which aims to communicate a defined linear story through archetypes and plain writing. With lit fic, mastery of the language and an eye for compelling conflict usually outweigh plot; with genre fiction, plot-and-conflict alignment usually triumphs over literary elegance. It's difficult for emerging writers to break into literary fiction unless they've developed a technically precise style that aligns to contemporary program-fiction standards and practices.
2. *Some genres are more amenable to cancel culture than others.* Given that the industry as a whole skews overwhelmingly progressive, it's not a surprise that some genres—young-adult and children's books lead the pack—embrace identity politics. Certain hot-button issues like race, class, sex, gender expression, sexual orientation, disability, and the like, must often reflect the progressive consensus *and* be written by people with "lived experience" with those issues. It's undoubtedly true that the industry has made significant errors of judgment at the expense of minority-perspective writers and poets. However, a small but loud cadre of self-appointed Twitter activists have proven effective at bullying some major publishers into ideological compliance. As an emerging writer, crossing these political lines may prove perilous to your literary career.
3. *Don't chase the rainbow.* Today's glut of bestselling content will almost surely cool by the time you develop a story idea, write it, and shop it. Generally speaking, industry execs know what's in the pipeline for the next 18 months. If you anticipate a trend—new variations of the sparkly vampire, dystopian epics with strong female main characters, #OwnVoices narratives, North Korean bad guys, naïve boy wizards, men bonding with their dogs, reinterpretations of the War of the Roses—you may get lucky and meet a market need even if your manuscript isn't immaculate. But given how long books take to write and publish, you'd have to anticipate the theme before it became a theme, so the odds aren't in your favor. By the time the theme's established in conventional-reader markets, major publishers have already closed the window for new glom-on manuscripts.
4. *Historical fiction must be historically accurate.* Merely setting a story in a different time period isn't enough to cast it as *historical fiction*. Instead, the story must cohere tightly to the time period in question, including in terms of how characters behave. It's a common trope among emerging writers to take what amounts to a contemporary-fiction piece and set it in a different era. Editors search for plot-and-conflict disconnects relative to the era and aren't likely to contract stories or books that prove too discrepant. In particular, using a historical era to make a point about a modern political issue—e.g., setting a strong and independent village matron against an evil Medieval priest—presents challenges because the premise, even if plausible, reeks of historicism and didacticism.[7] Historical

7: Unless, of course, historicism and didacticism are your wheelhouse—in which case, carry on, although at this point you're not technically writing "historical fiction" anymore.

tropes deployed to make a modern political point almost always prove difficult to rehabilitate unless you specifically target small- or mid-sized presses with a self-professed political bent.

5. *You're not going to sell a hyperlocal memoir.* As a micro-press leader I saw a ton of memoirs or biographies about people of little-to-no meaningful repute. The story of your great-grandfather's heroic journey from the Old Country is probably beautiful and deeply moving, but it's not market viable if he passed away in obscurity a half-century ago. Likewise, a book-length treatment of some "famous within the county" landmark isn't market viable, either. People and places that aren't famous on a state or national level just aren't going to be of sufficient general interest to justify a commercial book contract; at best, they're best presented as short pieces targeted to local magazines.
6. *Highly experimental or deep-penetration styles constrain your market reach.* Most experimental or non-standard forms of prose writing generally follow lit-fic conventions; they're best deployed in short stories or short creative nonfiction. Sometimes a book-length treatment—e.g., *Angela's Ashes*—hits the market, but in most cases, these titles remain more acclaimed than read, more difficult than delightful. Most genre-fiction writers naturally avoid experimental styles but they often explore narrative approaches wherein the point-of-view character and the narrator blend into a single monotonal voice that functions like a first-person story using third-person pronouns. This mode of writing, called *deep penetration*, isn't intrinsically problematic, and it's common in some genres. But it's a wickedly difficult mode of writing to pull off well. Emerging authors are well-served to avoid deep penetration until they've achieved mastery of point-of-view and narrative voice.

4.4 Manuscript Formatting

When an author secures a contract with a large-sized publisher, it's almost always by means of a literary agent. At that level of complexity, either the agent or the publisher accepts an author's manuscript and prepares it for commercial use in ways that are often opaque to the author.

Authors sometimes pay little attention to how their manuscripts are formatted, particularly with behind-the-scenes document configuration. And with large presses, some anonymous, underpaid intern or document specialist will fix everything without drama. For smaller presses, though, the resources to fix a poorly formatted manuscript prove somewhat more dear. For that reason, it's helpful to understand best-practice standards so they can be incorporated during the initial drafting process. Relying on a small-press publisher to clean up a structurally deficient manuscript might be an assumption that weighs against you during the publisher's review of the slush pile.

Images and Typefaces

But first, a basic fact about book development: No publisher anywhere "prints" a book using Microsoft Word or Scrivener—two of the most common programs for novel writing. Instead, publishers of fiction use a powerful application like Adobe InDesign or Quark XPress to lay out the book using a frame-based design logic. That completed document exports to an antiquated version of the Adobe PDF standard,[8] which loads cleanly into the memory of a high-capacity, high-speed printer. Print jobs of fewer than 1,000 books are generally prepared using a digital printer (effectively, an oversized photocopier) while 1,000 or more books are usually printed by an offset printer, similar to how newspapers are produced, although this isn't a hard-and-fast rule and it's subject to a lot of financial asterisks. Either way, the computer that controls the printer requires not only the book's contents, as presented within the PDF, but also the supporting files that make the book possible.

8: The X1:2001 standard is typical.

Supporting files come in two flavors: Images and typefaces. Images typically must appear at 300 dots per inch. If the print job is black-and-white, then the image must be a true greyscale file; you cannot include a color image and then assume a monochrome printer will do the conversion work for you. If the print job is in color, then the image usually must inhabit the CMYK colorspace. CMYK stands for *cyan, magenta, yellow, and key*; this colorspace governs standard four-color printing.[9] It's the most common approach for printing on paper. The other colorspace, RGB, stands for *red, green, and blue*; it's most common for on-screen displays like websites and e-readers. Microsoft Word doesn't care about image resolution or colorspace, but programs like InDesign *preflight* (i.e., inspect) a file and return errors if a project intended for a commercial printer doesn't meet industry standards for commercial printing. For example, a book with a picture in it that uses the RGB colorspace will fail preflight; if the failure is overridden, the CMYK-based printer will print the image, but the colors won't match identically because they're defined differently.

9: When you see *key*, assume it means *black*.

Typefaces—also called *font families*—present a bit of a sticky wicket. Relatively few authors understand that the thing that Word has trained them to call a "font" is actually a typeface. Typefaces are the named collection of a series of related fonts. Usually, the font represents a variant within the typeface family. So the Times New Roman *typeface* includes a Roman, an Italic and a Boldface *font*. Microsoft Word doesn't treat a "font" the same way that commercial publishers treat a font or a typeface—more about which, below.

Format Conventions

Before we talk specifically about optimizing your use of Microsoft Word, let's review the basic rules of manuscript formatting regardless of the tool you use for drafting:

- The Rule That Supersedes All Other Rules is to conform to the requirements of the agent or editor with whom you're working. Specific house rules always trump generic industry practices. In initial drafting, you obviously won't conform to some as-yet unknown publisher's house rules, but as you're contracted and begin revision with an editor, your manuscript must align to the house stylebook. It's almost always safe, with fiction, to follow the conventions of *The Chicago Manual of Style*.

- Always assume 8.5-inch-by-11-inch paper in the United States or A4 in Europe and elsewhere. Apply 1-inch margins.[10]
- Begin the first chapter with an all-caps heading that begins one-third to one-half of the way down the page. It's usually not necessary to add this buffer spacing for subsequent chapters; starting them at the top of a new page is sufficient.
- Each new paragraph receives a half-inch indent. Don't use tabs or spaces—set the indention using the ruler.
- Use left-justified (not full-justified) paragraphs.
- Include a running header or footer that contains the page number, your last name and the title or abbreviated title of the book. Omit this head on the first page of the book.
- Use a serif typestyle in 11-point text. Common options include Times New Roman, Palatino, and Garamond. Stick with a typeface that's on your computer by default and avoid getting creative with typestyles. No one wants to see Comic Sans, for example. *No one.*
- Never insert discretionary line breaks to force paragraphing to fall a certain way. Paragraphing sees its final adjustment at the end of the layout process; it's not necessary to tweak it while you're drafting.
- Use a continuous break to force Word to the next page, to begin a new chapter. Don't rely on embedded line breaks.[11]
- Don't let your software auto-correct special characters like ellipses or em dashes. These characters generate during typesetting and layout, not during drafting.
- Avoid inserting superfluous material like tables of contents or little glyphs to separate scenes. A TOC generates after a book is laid out; it doesn't map to a manuscript in Word. Likewise, cover pages, dedications, about-the-author pages, and related material isn't part of the manuscript. Omit it. The stuff that comes before Chapter One and after The End isn't developed and inserted until the book is ready for layout.

10: This book was developed for A4, although it's not common to print books at standard letter or A4 sizes. Poets take note: A highly structured poem that takes full advantage of an 8.5-by-11 canvas almost surely will prove problematic for chapbooks and literary journals developed for smaller trim sizes.

11: In other words, use the `Insert Break` function, don't just pound the Return key a dozen times.

It used to be conventional to use a monospace typeface, like Courier or Inconsolata, and to render emphasized text in underline. That convention has long since been eclipsed by the transition from typewriters to word processors. It's not inherently wrong to follow this approach—Scrivener even features a compile setting for it—but it's no longer commonplace.

Typesetting Matters

Your Microsoft Word manuscript should be optimized for easy translation into a frame-based layout engine. The more you screw around with tabs and spaces and line breaks and cutesy glyphs to mimic the look of a book within your word processor, the more someone else must undo all this unnecessary tomfoolery. Certain non-fiction books don't use Word, however. They rely on advanced markup languages that automatically compile the book into a print-ready format in a process called *typesetting*. This book, for example, was developed using LaTeX—a venerable typesetting syntax that allows the book to compile according to a pleasing visual style without manual layout.

The Problem of Word

One reason that Microsoft Word, in the hands of non-power-users, is wickedly suboptimal for publishing is because Word is too permissive about typefaces. In Word, for example, you can write a sentence in XYZ "font" if you have XYZ "font" on your computer. If you later decide that the title should be italics, most authors just highlight the title and press `Ctrl+I` to make it italic. And presto! Word makes the sentence lean to the right. The challenge, though, is that you might not have an italic font of the XYZ typeface on your computer. Word doesn't care; programmatically, it just makes the "italic" stuff slanty. But commercial presses do care. If you cannot embed an italic variant of the font—e.g, a specific font called *XYZ Italic*—then a problem arises: The printer will not accept the resulting PDF for printing. It *can't* print; it doesn't have access to an XYZ Italic font embedded into the PDF.

Desktop printers intended for home or light business duty accept print jobs from programs like Word in the form of a photograph. I'm writing this chapter using my Microsoft Surface Pro 4. It's attached, wirelessly, to a Hewlett-Packard color Laser Jet Pro printer. If I were to print from Word, Windows 10 spools the print job as an image, which the Laser Jet reconstructs. You don't need a font if you have a picture of a font. But commercial presses don't work like that: *They need the font file, not just a picture of the text.*

Even beyond printing, the translation of Word documents into InDesign or Quark XPress sometimes opens frustrating gaps. For example, depending on how the Word document was developed, it's possible that a Word file imported into InDesign will lose all formatting. Love italics or boldface? Guess what—you're screwed.[12]

12: The advent of swiss-army-knife tools like Pandoc—a multiformat file converter—reduce the import stress with some of these documents, but glitches inevitably remain.

Unless you use Microsoft Word correctly.

Word is a powerful tool. Many wonderful novels have been composed using this industry-standard program. But to ensure that the document you write in Word is maximally useful to potential publishing partners, you must use Word more precisely than you would if you're just writing a letter to a friend.

A Scribble About Scrivener

Some power authors love Scrivener, the comprehensive writing program developed by Literature and Latte. Scrivener employs a complex under-the-hood document-management system that relies on individual Rich Text Format files mediated by a .SCRIV index. Publishers do not want Scrivener files. Instead, almost everyone in fiction markets relies on Word.

So, in Scrivener, you compile your novel to Word. However, agents and editors generally rely on Word's Track Changes feature to transmit edits and comments. So, Scrivener users, you may either "fork" your novel—i.e., transfer the authoritative version from Scrivener to Word—

or translate Word comments/edits line-by-line back to Scrivener. Your call. But using Word is pretty much not negotiable except in technical writing.

Best Practices for Word

Five best-practice conventions govern drafting in Word.

First, use Styles. More than any other activity, using Styles in Word helps your manuscript translate cleanly to other formats. At a minimum, you'll need three styles: one for body text, one for emphasized body text, and one for headers. For body text, configure it to use something like Times New Roman at 11-point type, with left-justified paragraphs and double spacing, with no extra spacing between paragraphs. For the emphasized body text, you'll base it on your main body text, but you'll change the font to *Times New Roman Italic*. The header style may be whatever you like—bold, or a sans-serif typestyle.

Here's the thing: All text in your story must conform to a Style. That lovely group of items in the Font section of the Word ribbon? Never, ever use them. Don't italicize by clicking `Ctrl+I` or highlighting text and pressing the slanted *I* button on the ribbon. Instead, apply your new emphasized-body-text Style. It's more cumbersome, and it's a violation of your long-established muscle memory, but it's the way that professional authors write. *See Figure 4.6.*

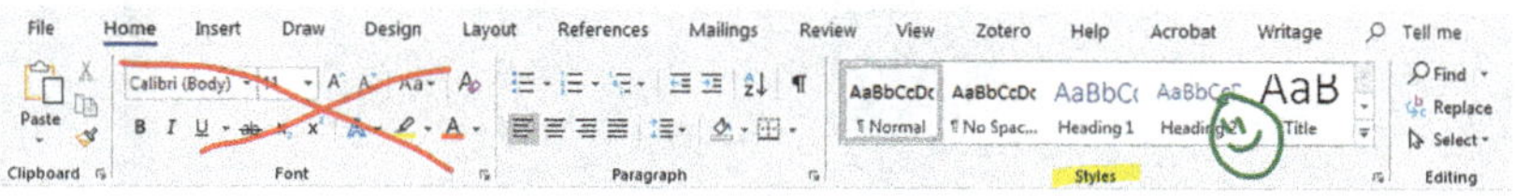

Figure 4.6: Use Word Styles, not the Font group!

Second, use hanging indents instead of tabs. Never use the tab key. If you prefer to see the text with the first paragraph intended, set a hanging first-line indent. In fact, make that indent part of your default body-text style. Superfluous tabs make layout more challenging, because book designers rely on hanging indents. Mixing between a hanging indent and a tab among different chapters makes for significant clean-up work after the fact.

Third, focus on content, not formatting. Your job, as the author, is to provide *text*. It's not to provide a *stylized document*. Don't waste time with fancy spacing options, changes to typefaces, drop-caps, or precise full-paragraph justification. The only formatting you'll provide is an indication of emphasis with italics, and those italics should be affected through a Style in Word. Novels do not use boldface, all caps, changes in point size, or adjustments to justification to provide emphasis. All you get are italics, so use them wisely![13]

13: And rarely, except for mental speech.

Fourth, use a citation manager. If you write non-fiction that requires academic references, use a citation manager like JabRef instead of hard-coding your citations in a Word bibliography. If, for example, you manually cited in MLA format but your press uses APA format, someone—maybe you, maybe a press employee—will have to manually reformat every citation. But with a proper citation manager, you can just click a different cite style and the bibliography will automagically reformat.

Fifth, reference—don't embed—images. Novelists don't include embedded imagery, but some writers of illustrated creative or technical non-fiction do. The convention is to reference something like `[Insert figure 4.3 here]` in the body text and let the book designers worry about sizing, spacing, and layout. Include the images as separate files with the manuscript file and ensure that they're labeled in a way that supports easy one-to-one association of your inline reference with the relevant image.

These five simple rules cover the most common errors afflicting Word files. You'll probably rarely go wrong if you remember the golden rule that *authors supply text, not print-ready documents* and any minimally necessary formatting they require to present the text is effected through Styles in Word.

Writing Tribes | 5

Tame your introvert. Without a good, high-functioning writers' group, you're cutting yourself off from one of the most vital tools in the aspiring author's toolbox. Deep and frequent engagement with a stable critique group isn't optional. In this chapter, we start with an essay about the perils of self-editing, followed by a study of beta readers. We end with 13 points for offering a critique and 11 points for receiving a critique and some standards for feedback and networking.

5.1 Layers of the Onion

Here's a dirty little secret about writing for publication: You cannot do it alone. Sure, you might sit in your special place—a coffee shop, a dedicated room in your house, a bench in the park, an Amtrak sleeper car, a National Park Service residency—and scribble in peace, by yourself, without distraction. For most people, manuscript development really is an individual act of creative beauty. But the solo generation of a manuscript isn't the end of the process. In fact, it's just the beginning.

You need a broad professional network to bolster your odds of success. Lone-wolf writers generally don't fare well in the market because editors know when the only previous eyeballs on your story were your own. Everyone makes telltale minor mistakes we're incapable of identifying on self edit, but which glow like nuclear waste when fresh eyes with different perspectives engage with the manuscript.

My nuclear waste? My first drafts tend to repeat the same 10-cent words in successive sentences and my commas proliferate like rabbits in a predator-free carrot patch. And when I get on a roll—i.e., when I plow through a section of text after the second martini—I deploy the passive voice with the reckless abandon of a parkour champion dancing atop the skyscrapers of New York City. And sometimes I over-indulge in mixed metaphors, and sometimes not even on purpose.

How do I know that my writing bears those traits of toxicity? Because my critique groups rarely fail to point them out, so now I'm primed to correct them on self-edit in ways I never would have caught *before* I built a relationship with my fellow scribes.

There's an old rule about editing: Every pass catches 80 percent of the errors remaining in the manuscript. If you're blind to some percentage of those errors, then it's likely that enough problems remain that your work will be kicked out early in the slush-pile editing, especially if you forego walking through comprehensive self-edit checklists. There's just too much good content out there looking for a home to take a chance on a query laden with obvious mechanical defects.

The solution? Start with your writing tribe—a critique group.

Consider: With what small cluster of fellow writers do you share ideas and chapters? When you painstakingly crafted your *magnum opus*, with whom did you share especially problematic scenes or seek advice about character or plot development? As you completed chapters, who looked at them? If your answer is either "no one" or "my Great Aunt Ethel who likes to read a lot," then the most critical network a writer relies upon hasn't helped you to hone your work product.

Beyond the tribe, consider a cohort of beta readers. These people aren't necessarily the members of your critique group. Rather, they're experienced writers in their own right, competent to evaluate work in your genre and within your targeted length, but who aren't as familiar with your style as members of your critique group. A beta reader will look at the whole manuscript and offer feedback—not necessarily edits, but comments sufficient to help you figure out if you're on the right track. Beta readers are especially useful for reviewing detailed novel synopses.

Armed with a tribe and a circle of beta readers, you'll be better equipped to move to the next layer out: Peer authors. Network with other local writers! Attend book launches and poetry readings and literary mixers. Get to know the people who also write in your community, even if you don't share work with each other. A handful of peer authors turning a megaphone toward their own readers powerfully augments your reach when you need to promote your book, yet those other authors aren't going to market for you if they've never met you. If they know you, like you, and trust you, they'll be there for you—especially if you're also there for them. Peer relationships are always a two-way street.

Beyond fellows authors, your next layer out includes editors, agents, and publishers. Publishing can be a remarkably inbred affair. The larger the press, the more likely it is that a manuscript is considered not because it came out of the slush pile, but because it was advocated through word-of-mouth referral or through rainmaker or alumni relationships. For the largest presses, authors cannot even submit a query package; the big New York publishers work exclusively with agents. And within the agent world, the more seasoned the agent, the harder it is to obtain that agent's representation. Your query package must be *flawless* to get any attention at all unless you happen to know the right cousin or ex-girlfriend or former professor or whatever.

The outermost layer of the onion, of course, is the general book-buying public. Readers are a fickle lot, but you can't access them until you've worked through all the inner layers.

Early-career authors sometimes resist peer networking. They aspire to move their story from their laptop directly to the general reading public. Many times, they're introverted—a characteristic of writers!—and resist or resent the imperative to grow the onion large enough to meaningfully flavor the manuscript. The problem with this approach is that you'll likely remain invisible in your own community, and the work product you push along will not be as strong as it could have been, had you taken seriously the value of a critique group and a circle of beta readers.

The moral of the story: *Writing may be a solitary exercise, but being a published author requires a supportive community*. You cannot short-circuit the path from your desktop printer to the bookstore shelf. You must deliberately plan for your success.

5.2 Beta Readers

Beta readers have always served as a professional writer's best protection against misaligned expectations about the quality of his or her work. They come in two flavors: Persistent and transient. Persistent beta readers are usually just called *critique groups* whereas the transient ones typically consist of individual peer writers willing to do you a favor in exchange for future reciprocity.

It's not okay to ask your Great Aunt Ethel to serve as your beta reader. Always pick people who are *writers*. Every now and then, I receive cover letters containing statements that the author's mom/sister/aunt/cousin "who likes to read" thought the manuscript was great. As accolades go, that's weak sauce unless said mom/sister/aunt/cousin happened to be Margaret Atwood and she included her endorsement as a signed letter within the query package.

Critique Groups

A good critique group networks a stable, small number of people—six to eight is good; more than 10 proves too unwieldy—who are reasonably competent writers in their own right. A critique group is a significant long-term investment. The best ones meet weekly or semimonthly for several hours at a time. They conduct focused critiques of members' work and discuss craft and share practical advice for resolving the vexing literary problems of the day.

Avoid critique groups that meet monthly or less often or which consist of mostly inexperienced writers. You're welcome to join them, perhaps as a mentor or for the social value, but they're unlikely to give you meaningful feedback relative to your time investment.[1] Likewise, groups with open membership, for which you can't predict who will be present at any given meeting, foreclose meaningful relationship building that helps others grow familiar with your voice and goals and therefore optimize the feedback they offer.

1: I participate in a monthly social confab of writers who eat pizza and sometimes play writing-related games. It's a ton of fun, but it's more "friend group" than "critique group." Writing-related friend groups are wonderful, but they don't meet the definition of *critique group* as advanced in this book.

If you can't get a substantive critique on a chapter or two at least once every other month, then you'd be well advised to find an alternative group. Likewise, if the feedback you receive is superficial—nothing written, or comments that suggest your colleagues didn't read, or read only once, your piece before the meeting—then the group is similarly sub-optimal.

It's helpful to ensure that at least some members of the group enjoy some expertise with your genres and your typical story length. If you write epic fantasies, for example, a group of literary-fiction short-story writers will be of value, but not nearly as much value as a group of fantasy writers or novel writers would be. It's okay to ask about the background and experience of group members when you ask to join, or are invited to join, a critique group; joining the wrong group may be more harmful than not joining a group at all.[2]

2: Can't find a group? Your local library system might help, or join a virtual group. Online groups aren't as helpful as in-person meetings, but they're better than nothing.

Relationship Maintenance

Because a critique group is the core of your support system, your success depends on large part on how you relate to the rest of the team.

For starters, understand that the group is a *community*. They'll help you, but you must help them. If you're one member of a group of seven, then you'll end up six-parts giving to one-part receiving. That ratio doesn't work in your favor, unless that one-seventh slice that you obtain is well-optimized to help you advance your craft and to keep you motivated when you're imprisoned in a maze of writers blocks.

So how do you optimize it?

First, work with partners who align to your specific level of experience, your writing level, and your genre. The closer your group's skill level touches on the stuff you actually write, the more useful their observations become. Although it's not helpful to have a group filled with people who only write the same thing—outside perspectives matter—a balance of some-who-do and some-who-don't ensure you encounter several different interpretations of your work. The Goldilocks Principle governs, to some degree.

Second, insist that everyone in the group pulls his or her own weight. If some people habitually decline to fully engage with critiques, they're free-riding. It's okay to ask whether low-engaged members provide net value or merely fill a seat that someone else could more profitably occupy. When a critical mass of members develops a rotating list of excuses why they can't show up or couldn't get the work done, it's time to rethink the group and its membership.

Third, watch for groups with people who habitually reject feedback. A certain type of writer likes to attend critique sessions to read his or her work and to listen to praise. You know the type: As soon as someone offers a suggestion for improvement, the author interrupts with explanations that dismiss the suggestion and undermine the person who made it. Eventually, people learn to either pull their punches or to not even bother with substantive engagement. That passive-aggressive dynamic is a death knell for a well-functioning group. Channel those people out.

Fourth, find groups where education and shared goal accountability—and not just rote review—works into the warp and weft of the group's ethos. Critiques are good, but it's even better if every now and then a member of the group takes accountability for developing some targeted education session, or if the group issues internal challenges to write things, or tracks in a shared space everyone's annual goals and individual progress toward them. Fine-tuning your technique is hard, and although critiques help, they're only part of the solution. A framework for mutual accountability works wonders for keeping people motivated and on the right path.

Fifth, ensure that everyone's aligned as to long-term career goals. A person who wants to write short stories to shop to lit journals because he wants to join an MFA program is different from a person who only *really* writes during National Novel Writing Month. Everyone doesn't have to have the same goal, but it's helpful when everyone's goals share at least some degree of overlap.

Finally, look for compatibility of outlook. It's not terribly unusual for people who might be compatible on paper to disintegrate as a unit because they don't see eye-to-eye on subjects like politics and religion, when people in the group tend to write politically or religiously engaged stories. Although viewpoint diversity is intrinsically valuable, its also hard for some people to put their ideology aside to offer good-faith critiques of content that hails from a different perspective.

Whenever you join an existing group or accept members into a new one that you've founded, it's fair to ask pointed questions and to request writing samples. The value of a critique group isn't just checking the box of having one—rather, the value lies in its goodness-of-fit relative to your goals and levels of experience. An ill-fitting or outright toxic group, then, is no better (and often worse) than no group at all.

5.3 13 Points for Peer Critiquing

Your primary goal as a reviewer is to help the author to improve his or her manuscript. A critique session is not an opportunity for you to boast of superior knowledge or skill or to assert your own ideas for alternative plot points. Because most critiques are subjective, it's incumbent upon the reviewer to present feedback in a way that reduces the risk of emotional harm to the author.

This point is significant: Your task is to help the author improve the manuscript in light of the author's natural voice and goals. The worst critiques come from a place that says, "Had I been the author, I would have written it differently." The most toxic critique partners substitute their own preferences, style, and voice for the author's. Such an approach serves no one's best interests.

A bakers' dozen of critique principles seem to work well.

Obtain appropriate context before you begin a critique. You cannot help the author if you don't understand where the author's at in the process and what he or she needs to advance the draft. At a minimum, you should clarify what you've been given to review (Full story? First chapter? Scene from mid-book?) and what kind of critique the author's looking for. It's also helpful to understand external constraints, like word-count or point-of-view requirements or mandatory thematic elements (e.g., for a literary contest) or expected audiences. If the author doesn't supply this context, ask for it. It's never fair to invest time in a blind reading when the author's only really after one or two bits of undisclosed feedback.

Read before you review. Engage the content from start to finish before marking up your copy or taking notes. You won't find plot errors early in the piece until you get to the end of the piece, for example, so don't diminish the value of your critique by being too hasty.

Find nice things to say. A critique that emphasizes the negative with very few words of praise not only stings the author, but if this negative mode becomes a habit, you'll find your peers more likely to dismiss your feedback over the long run. Although critiques address specific work products, critiquing in general also becomes an exercise in long-term peer networking and relationship building. People don't generally enjoy hanging around the persistently negative.

Don't hedge your bets. Say what you need to say—no more and no less. It's not helpful to caveat statements with qualifiers like "that's just my opinion" or "maybe I'm confused." Not only do those comments imply passive-aggressive snark but they also undermine your authority as a reviewer.

Find solutions, not problems. It's far less helpful to an author to be told that some plot point "doesn't work" than to receive feedback that the point "might work better if" some alternative approach were employed. You'll find that offering solutions helps to minimize the overall negativity of your critique. Plus, a solution contextualizes your concern and gives the author at least a starting point for revision.

Own your feedback. As a reviewer, your task is to share your reaction to an author's work product. As such, you speak solely for yourself—you don't speak for all readers—and much of what you share is subjective. Using *I* statements instead of *you* statements when expressing an opinion will therefore honor the relationship between author and reviewer. For example, write "I think this scene would flow more smoothly if it had more cowbell because . . . " instead of "you should add more cowbell" or "readers want more cowbell" or "this scene doesn't work."

The point is important enough to bear repeating: *You don't speak for all readers.* So avoid generalizing your feedback. If you don't like a passage, for example, then say so. It's disingenuous to suggest that "most readers" won't like it.[3]

3: Unless you can point to a published, peer-reviewed study that establishes the point.

Focus on structure, not minutiae. Help the author to reposition the big rocks rather than fretting about the pebbles and the grains of sand. Incidental foibles are best left for written feedback. It's painful to watch a critique group break into squabbling about the minor details of a story, especially regarding trivial facts or minor continuity glitches. Experienced members usually spot the people who didn't do their homework because, in lieu of contemplating big-picture structural suggestions, they seize upon some nugget of trivia and beat it to death with a sledgehammer.

The pattern really does seem to hold. Reviewers who offer little-to-no written feedback and belabor trivial points in an oral critique (e.g., word use, an apparent factual inconsistency, a minor description imprecision) almost surely didn't prepare in advance. This phenomenon is well-known in university seminar rooms. You cannot fake a structural critique by executing a panicked, surreptitious first read at the start of the feedback session. Thus, people whose feedback is always focused at the line level and never at the structure level are the very same people who aren't pulling their own weight in the group.

Present detailed syntax corrections in written form. Although it's sometimes fair in a group discussion to mention one or two grammar or usage points that many authors consistently get wrong, let your marked-up copy (returned to the author) offer the specifics. Calling out minor mistakes or a large number of line errors, in the context of the oral component of a group peer review, is bad manners.

Minimize the violence against the author's intent. As a reviewer, you will encounter styles different from your own. Your task is to honor the style and intent of the author. In particular, claims about the depth of characters, the quantity of scene descriptions, or the choice of words are open to the "well, if I had done it, I would have done *X* instead" construct. The less violence you inflict on the author's original vision, the more likely it is that the author will give your suggestions a fair evaluation. Ask yourself: Is a point of feedback specifically actionable by the receiving author, or is it your subjective statement that offers no meaningful direction for potential improvements? If the former, great. If the latter, consider leaving that hobbyhorse in the stable.

Relatedly, some authors and genres prove more amenable to polysyllabic diction than others. For example, a space opera might be written at a 12th-grade level, but literary fiction need not be so constrained. The appropriateness of "big words" with more complex sentence structures is highly context dependent, but it's not true that "big words" are always disfavored.

Hop over the bunny holes. Check for conformance to genre norms and that the plot follows an expected arc, but think twice before suggesting side stories. Inexperienced reviewers sometimes go down plot bunny holes such that the bulk of their critiques are either what-if scenarios within the plot or alternatives to how scenes unfolded (sometimes unhelpfully couched in terms of generic readers being "drawn in" or "drawn out"). Especially with short stories and samples from novels, avoid the tendency to make the plot or the characters do more than what's necessary to make the story succeed on its own terms.[4]

4: Except when you're reviewing a synopsis rather than a story, or if the person you're critiquing specifically requests alternatives to a given plot point.

Leave some strings untied. Resist the urge to close every loop if the story doesn't require it. Authors need not make all aspects of the story comprehensible to the lowest common denominator of generic readers. Toleration for ambiguity often proves stronger among lit-fic writers than among genre-fiction writers. It's okay to leave some facts vague or some resolutions imperfect, if that's the overall direction the author intends. People who belabor minor loose ends are often the same people who either didn't prepare in advance or tend to write black-and-white "plot-driven" stories.

Research what you don't understand. If the author introduces vocabulary or ideas or allusions with which you're unfamiliar, it's never appropriate to suggest that the author's audience targeting is *ipso facto* inappropriate. Rather, take the time to study the language and the concepts—and only then raise the point, if (now informed) you think the targeting is off.

Likewise, do not flag facts within a story unless you're sure that the fact is inaccurate. Instead of suggesting that "I don't think it works this way," instead offer an authoritative description of what's true. Never fake competence, and don't interject speculation or suggestions that the author research something more deeply in lieu of you researching it on the author's behalf.

Do your job. Critiquing well takes time. You cannot do it 10 minutes before your writing group convenes or ad-lib it during a face-to-face session. You'll likely need to read the material several times to prepare well-considered suggestions that will empower the author to enhance the manuscript. This curation effort means you may discard valid observations that you know will not be well-received to avoid the author shutting out your feedback altogether. In other words: Pick your battles with care. If Fate precluded you from preparing adequately before a critique session, own up to it and *do not speak during the critique session*. Life, after all, includes many priorities that outrank uncompensated peer review. Each writing group, however, must set its own baseline standard for how often this unpreparedness manifests before someone is asked to step down. Consider the lack of an accountability framework as a giant red flag about the long-term viability of the group.

5.4 11 Points for Being Critiqued

DESPITE THE PAIN OF BEING REVIEWED, accept both praise and criticism as a gift on your lifelong journey of perfecting your craft.

Eleven points govern.

Identify yourself. Put your name on your story, and give the story some sort of title, even if it's just a working one for the purpose of the critique. The only exception is when the story, by prior agreement, obtains a blind read. Few things prove as vexing to people who edit by hand than to print several stories for review and then they must figure out who wrote what, and which pages apply to which story.

Format the story correctly. It's good practice to share documents that are correctly formatted for print, even if most people annotate electronically. As such, use a minimum of 1-inch margins on all sides, double spaced, with no extra spaces between paragraphs. Use an 11- or 12-point serif typeface (like Times New Roman or Palatino). It's *never* acceptable to submit single-spaced documents or stories with butt-ugly typefaces like Comic Papyrus.[5] Likewise, every file should include a running header with your last name, the page number, and either the story title or an

5: I once received a short-story submission written in 16-point Comic Papyrus, shaded in violet.

abbreviation thereof. The only exception to the format-as-if-its-printed rule applies when online or electronic editing is mandatory by prior agreement. And even then, adequate spacing, point size, and margins contribute to on-screen legibility.[6]

6: See Chapter 4 for additional context about formatting standards.

Offer useable documents. It's usually safe to send Microsoft Word or Adobe PDF documents; it's riskier to send people OpenOffice documents or InCopy files or even plain-text files. Do not make people click links into cloud-storage services unless—by prior agreement—you're committing your work to a collaborative-editing environment like GitHub or OneDrive or a Google Doc. The file should be accessible and should support tools like PDF comments or Track Changes comments if the critique partner prefers electronic editing, so don't apply security settings to the file to lock down edits.

Provide context. Offer a brief setup for a scene so the reviewer enjoys appropriate context for his or her comments. It's not helpful to ask a reviewer to read blindly, particularly from the middle of a larger project. Supply this context as part of your package to your reviewers. Especially for scenes in the middle of a book, informing or reminding your critique partners of where you're at in the story helps to avoid peripheral questions that arise solely because the reader lacks situational awareness.

Ask for help. It's rarely helpful to offer a story or scene without indicating why you presented that piece. Do you struggle with characterization? Or plausibility? Or world-building? Or grammar? It's totally legit to say, "I'm having trouble with X and would really like some advice." Otherwise, the feedback you'll get will, inevitably, be a Rorschach test. Likewise, it's great to tell people you're not interested in deep grammar-and-usage review because the draft will likely substantively change. Your readers will appreciate your permission to avoid doing the unnecessary![7]

7: The only time it's helpful to not lodge a specific ask is when you think it's done-done and ready to shop.

Clarify, don't confront. If a reviewer offers feedback that you think misses the boat, it's better to say something like "I intended to do X, but it sounds like you think I didn't fully achieve that goal, so how do you think I could close the gap?" instead of arguing with the reviewer. Savvy reviewers generally figure out which authors will argue and then shy away from offering them their most nuanced and useful guidance. But asking for help in fixing the problem puts the onus on the reviewers to more fully articulate their position—and even if you think a reviewer is off-base, you'll have better insight into how your story might nevertheless be tightened.

Avoid explanations. If a reviewer is confused about a plot point, resist the temptation to explain it. Instead, make a note to address the point of confusion in the text because it's likely that other readers will react similarly. If you must explain it to one person, you'll need to explain it to many, so *edit* instead of *defend*.

Consider the consensus. As an author, you're always free to reject the counsel of others, but if there's an independent consensus about a point, it's probably prudent to concede.

Say "thank you." Many professional authors never actually speak during critiques of their work, except at the end, when they offer their thanks; they observe the critique rather than participate in it, taking notes and thinking about the story instead of planning their next rebuttal. Always express your gratitude for the reviews, even when you're not fully satisfied with the session. Gratitude builds relationships that transcend individual speed bumps.

Zip Your Lips

Each peer group adopts its own conventions, but you'd be well served to observe the no-talking rule when your own work is under review. There's something useful in watching others discuss your work without you stepping in every three seconds to argue or defend. You learn a lot more by keeping your mouth closed and your ears open, compared to the reverse.

Follow up. Apply the feedback from the critique session to your story within a few days of having received it. Your reviewers took the time to give you advice; the least you can do is revise the story considering their comments! Particularly when the advice is still fresh in your mind.

Don't take it personally. No matter how indelicate the feedback may be, remember that the reviewer is speaking to your story and not to you as a human or to you as an author. Even when it feels as if your story were viciously hacked with a meat cleaver, remember that each round of revision makes the story stronger. And remember, too, that being blindsided by harsh feedback suggests you are too close to the story to see its potential flaws. Instead of being angry or hurt, and therefore amenable to rejecting all the feedback, set everything aside for a few weeks then come back to it with fresh eyes. A little "social distancing" from your own stories works wonders for resetting your good cheer.

5.5 Modes of Feedback

You'll engage in critiques in at least one of three ways—orally, in paper form. or in electronic form. And you'll engage the material either in advance, or as a cold read in a group setting. The methods and lead time influence the best way to deliver your comments.

In a cold read—in which, you don't see the material until the session starts—the best you can do is look at material from a line level, throwing in observations about structure as opportunities arise. A line-level analysis looks at the content from the perspective of sentences and paragraphs. You're critiquing mechanics, primarily, and things like characterization, diction, pacing, and tone. Because you can't sit with it to ponder the story, your feedback on high-level structure will necessarily be hit-or-miss, but offer what you can. A lot of cold-read feedback is impressionistic rather than deeply reasoned. And that's okay. This type of session, performed in a group, functions generatively; as people make observations, others build upon them, so that real insight often follows.

With lead time, however, you've rarely got an excuse to avoid a structural review. The more time you have, the higher-level your assessment should aim. The best critiques look at the story from 50,000 feet to verify genre conformance, plot coherence, plot-conflict alignment, plausibility, and related subjects; it spends less time at the level of individual sentences. The more lead time you enjoy, the less you should obsess about proofreading unless the requestor specifically asks for it.[8]

8: Especially with a story under active development, there's little point to word-smithing text that'll likely change several more times before final-draft status. So don't waste the energy!

During the delivery of the critique, you'll usually share feedback face-to-face with the author. Use that time well—mention a few things you thought worked really well and mention a few things that you thought could be improved, *and suggest what those improvements might look like*. Never belabor grammar quibbles or minor factual points in an oral session. And you don't need to treat the oral session like a recitation of your written critique notes. Delivering a summary of your high-level observations suffices.

During the critique session, you'll almost always deliver written notes to the author. When you're working in a real-time collaboration environment, like Google Docs, your comments stamp into the work as it unfolds. If you engage the material in advance, you generally get to pick your poison—handwritten or electronic notes.

Written feedback follows three channels. One consists of simple proof-reading. Those edits incorporate directly into the text, either through proofreaders' marks or through actual edits to the source material in a Track Changes mode. The only time you leave comments about proof-reading is when you can't edit—for example, when you work from a PDF. The second channel consists of observations at a line level. Those generally run as comments in both a PDF document or a Word document. The third channel consists of summary notes. Those append to the bottom of the file, as new paragraphs in their own right, not connected to any particular passage. Alternatively, the summary may appear as a separate document or a reply to an email or to a forum post.

Critique Checklist

As you progress through a given story, ask questions about how it unfolds:

- What's the main conflict? Does it inform and guide the plot? Does it make sense? Is it resolved by the end of the story?
- Does the story conform to genre norms? Does the plot make sense? Are major touchpoints appropriately spaced?
- Is the point-of-view mode right for the story? Are there too many or too few POV characters? Is it clear which POV governs a given story unit? Was the optimal POV character selected for a given story unit?

- Does the story advance an archetypical theme? Any jarring inconsistencies with voice at a character, narration, or whole-story level?
- Does conflict interweave the storyline? Is the reader eager to turn the page to find out what happens next?
- Do characters feel distinct? Are they well-considered? Do conflicts and motivations seem plausible and multi-dimensional?
- Are descriptions limited to what's relevant in the moment? Is there too much backstory? Is there too little description given the context? Are the same traits hammered again and again? Are there too many stage directions?
- Is it clear how the narrator disambiguates from the POV character? Does the narration match the POV? Is author intrusion limited?
- Is there an appropriate balance of dialogue to action? Does each character speak with a unique voice? Do conversations make sense?
- Do chapters and scenes make sense? Do things end and begin where they ought? Does the story as a whole begin and end where it should?
- Is the writing clear, concise, and free of grammar errors? Does word choice and sentence structure align to the target audience?
- Did you enjoy it? Did it offer a good emotional payoff?

No need to specifically call all these elements out in your critiques. Just thinking comprehensively about all the things you could address is enough to cover the bases.

5.6 Beta-Reader Networks

Critique groups rarely address novel-length materials in one sitting. For that type and intensity of engagement, you'll recruit individual writers who may be willing to spend 20 to 40 hours over four to six weeks to read your novel from start to finish then offer their detailed notes.

Professional networking will serve you well. A busy author is almost surely going to refuse a cold-call request for a beta read for a stranger, but a peer colleague may prove more amenable.

The most typical circumstance for this kind of heavy-lift review outside of a critique group relates to an *advance review copy* of a forthcoming book. ARCs are the last step in a book's development—they're the print-ready version of a book that's enjoying one last round of external review, both to tighten remaining glitches and to serve as promos for reviewers.

You'll sometimes find that authors who are part of various online communities prove willing to perform occasional beta reads. Do your research. Perhaps the one situation you should avoid is the review-trade deal, where two writers trade books in exchange for a "fair review" on Amazon. In this case, the author will review your manuscript-in-progress if you read a recently published book and review it on Amazon or Goodreads. There's nothing inherently wrong with this process, but some authors, particularly self- or vanity-published writers, use this approach to inflate their rankings, and as such, you should rightfully consider whether you're really going to receive as good as you get.

Never pay for a peer review. If you're going to pony up cash for a review, execute a contract with a professional book editor.

Reference Materials 6

Every author needs a shelf of trusty reference books. These dusty artifacts of leather, glue, paper, and coffee stains never go offline.

6.1 Dog-Eared Serendipity

Many authors swear by their collected websites and electronic tools. And these resources are, undoubtedly, useful. Yet the value of a printed reference book is that you browse its index or table of contents at a glance. So, yes, keep your browser bookmarks ready. But five interrelated premises suggest that a paper-first logic model may prove more useful in the long run.

First, a book is almost always better curated than a website. The Web is optimized for short-form, easily edited content and most sites don't require in-depth fact-checking or expertise before publication. A printed reference book released by a major press is presumed authoritative, however, because it incurred several rounds of fact-checking by recognized industry experts.

Quotation sites are a great case in point—many of these sites list all sorts of quotes with little formal curation and many of the quotes admit to dubious authenticity. If you want a recognized, authoritative quote, check *Bartlett's;* if you just want to appear intellectual-ish, accuracy notwithstanding, check *EliteQuoteMonster4U.com*.

Even a well-respected, deeply curated website—like Purdue University's Online Writing Lab—doesn't hold a candle to the depth and breadth of a print resource like *Garner's Modern English Usage*.

Second, websites offer a mishmash of information that may not cohere to a more focused logic model. A great example of this trend are the million-and-one blog posts about punctuation. Some sites do a better job of it than others, but the onus is on the author to verify timeliness of content and the assumptions that went into the blog post. The way you punctuate a manuscript using Associated Press standards, which are common for short-form technical and journalistic content, differ from the literary and academic standards in the *Chicago Manual of Style*, but if you don't understand the difference between AP and Chicago, you have no mental map for parsing the recommended usage patterns or recognizing why different online authorities deliver different answers. It's better to just refer to the AP's stylebook or to Chicago directly than to sort through which is which, and which revision of those sources the site relies upon.

Put differently: Websites are a great memory jogger for stuff you already basically know but just need to refresh. But if you don't know what you're looking for, the odds are low that you'll find what you really need.

Third, books don't require paywalls or subscriptions. Although you must invest in the book up front, once you own it, you own it. You need not pay monthly or annual subscriptions to a service that, in the long run, costs far more than the book did. You'll learn more from consulting authoritative grammar texts, for example, than by subscribing to a service like Grammarly and blindly allowing its algorithm to "correct" your language.[1]

1: It's always better to know what you're doing than to let a computer tell you what to do. Computers are great at flagging routine errors—like typos—but struggle with stuff like homonyms and tone. Never agree to a computer-generated change unless you understand why the flag appeared. In my writing, for example, roughly 20 percent of highlighted mistakes in Grammarly or Microsoft Word aren't actually errors, and in some cases blindly following the advice would *introduce* errors that weren't previously there.

Fourth, it's easier to cross-compare minutiae among reference books than among websites. Consider the long-running argument about using *over* synonymously with *more than*. A search on Google or Bing uncovers many different opinions stated with varying degrees of certitude and competence. But if you decamped to your reference library, you'd discover that:

- The Associated Press, starting in 2014, allowed *over* synonymously with *more than*. (In 2013 and earlier, this usage was explicitly disfavored.) However, the 1999 edition of *The New York Times Manual of Style and Usage* doesn't even address the question.
- The third edition of *The New Fowler's Modern English Usage* cautions against this usage.
- The fourth edition of *Garner's Modern American Usage* fully endorses this usage.
- The fifth edition of *Webster's New World College Dictionary* allows the usage, but only at the 14th lexical entry. Which is code for "you sure about that, buddy?"

Using *over* interchangeably with *more than* isn't an obvious error—it's arguably not an error at all[2] —but conservative authorities aren't fully on board with it. This interpretation of the usage pattern, at a meta level, sources from a review of the usage entries across several print books, not from any random curmudgeon's personal opinion that happened to rank high enough in the Search Engine Results Page.

2: Many disagreements about grammar address more-or-less optimal usage patterns rather than objectively correct patterns.

Finally, and perhaps most importantly, print materials support serendipitous learning. When you open a browser session to ask the question `should I use over or more than`, you'll read a bunch of answers of varying quality over that specific subject. But when I cracked open *Garner's* to verify the *over* entry, my eyes inadvertently alighted upon a nearby record:

> **outsized; outsize; adj.** The first is standard [American English]. The second is standard [British English].

Who knew?

This serendipity is precisely the point. As we discussed in Chapter 2 regarding your preparation goals for January, acquiring reference books and then orienting yourself to them is a critical first step in preparing to write. Just buying them and shelving them does you no good at all. Instead, you must inspect them in detail.

Spend an hour or so with each book. Familiarize yourself, deeply, with the table of contents. Then slowly flip through the text to get a feel for what each section offers. Build a mental map of what's covered in each book, *so you know when it's appropriate to check it in the future*.

Don't bother reading them; they're not designed to be engaging page-turners. The only time I read a reference book cover-to-cover was when I worked as a newspaper copy chief. I kept two copies of the AP stylebook—one at my desk, and the other in my car. In those days I did a lot of driving, and hence of eating meals in the driver's seat. I'd sit in the parking lot, munch a burger, and read a few more entries from the stylebook, starting with A and ending with Z. But, newspaper editing was my day job.

Admittedly, I leaned a lot from the AP that I didn't know I didn't know, but for most writers, simply remaining aware that these resources exist—and knowing them well enough to recognize when to consult them—should prove significantly more useful than relying on hit-or-miss websites.

6.2 Resource List

Consider buying some or all of the following 27 books and reviewing them in detail. They're presented in alphabetical order.

Disclaimer

I own each of these books. I recommend them because of their intrinsic value; I maintain no personal or professional relationship with the authors of these books, nor derive any sort of financial benefit from listing them.

The Associated Press Stylebook Every year, the Associated Press releases a new stylebook that melds style conventions with in-depth treatments of media law for journalists as well as special sections about subjects including social media and wire copy. The AP's manual governs journalism and much short-form stuff like online articles, although it's less common for novels. Buy a copy straight from AP, but you need not refresh yourself annually; the number of entries that turn over each year are generally small enough that buying fresh every other or every third year should prove sufficient. Nevertheless, the AP's books, because they support active journalists, usually represent cutting-edge decisions about usage and spelling, especially for proper nouns related to newsworthy people and places.[3]

3: The AP's conventions, because they're intended for journalistic settings where every superfluous character counts, forbid the serial comma (the so-called Oxford Comma) and the proliferation of acronyms in parentheses. In the fiction space, AP's conventions are less common; in technical writing, they're more common.

Bartlett's Familiar Quotations Bartlett's comes in many different styles and formats, but the gist is the same: You'll encounter quotes organized around indices of keywords. The value to owning a printed copy is that the contents of the book have been vetted by experts, so you can be reasonably sure that the quote is accurate and attributable to the source. As George Washington once said, "I cannot tell a lie—you cannot believe every quote you see on the Internet or on Goodreads." Many versions of varying lengths of this reference book dot the market. Pick one.

Between You and Me Mary Norris, a three-decade veteran of the copy shop at *The New Yorker*, writes a fast-paced, funny take on spelling and punctuation. The book is written as a narrative, not as a rulebook, and many of the examples touch on hot points in modern usage. The overall tone is one of "strictly permissive," an interesting square she circled with aplomb. Norton, 2015, ISBN 978-0-393-35214-6.

Bird by Bird Anne Lamont's classic book of writing inspiration is part literary memoir and part non-technical writing advice. It's an easy read that's as emotionally satisfying as it is intellectually stimulating. Pantheon Books, 1994, ISBN 978-0-385-48001-7.

The Business of Being a Writer Some people don't just want to write, they want to quit their day job to write. Jane Friedman, formerly a leader at *Writers Digest*, eschews the craft advice to focus on the business: In five sections ("First Steps," "Understanding the Publishing Industry," "Getting Published," "The Writer as Entrepreneur," "How Writers Make Money") she dives into the state of the industry and how writers—there's a glut of them, driving down prices—can nevertheless thrive. She doesn't sugarcoat your odds of success, though, despite offering some of the most insightful business-of-writing advice about today's market. University of Chicago Press, 2018, ISBN 978-0-226-39316-2.

The Chicago Guide to Grammar, Usage, and Punctuation Bryan A. Garner's complimentary volume to *The Chicago Manual of Style* elaborates in minute detail various English parts of speech, syntax considerations, sentence diagrams, word formation, word usage, and punctuation. A hefty tome, targeted to serious students of grammar. University of Chicago Press, 2016, ISBN 978-0-226-18885-0.

The Chicago Manual of Style This magisterial tome is *the* authoritative reference for most writers. Now in its seventeenth edition, *Chicago* presents more than 1,100 dense pages of content driven by three broad subjects. The first part, "The Publishing Process," includes technical guidance about manuscript formatting, rights, illustrations and tables, and proofreading. The second part, "Style and Usage," covers grammar, punctuation, spelling, names, titles, numbers, abbreviations, math, and quotations; this revision was heavily influenced by Bryan A. Gardner, who wrote two of the other books on this list—he's the leading authority on English usage currently drawing breath. The third and final part covers sources, citations, references, and indices. University of Chicago Press, 2017 (17th ed.), ISBN 978-0-226-28705-8.

Common Errors in English Usage Originally a list on the Internet, English professor Paul Brians eventually released it in book form. Similar in approach to any of several dozen "use this word not that one" books, *Common Errors* presents a straightforward, alphabetized list of words that are commonly misspelled, confused, misused, or otherwise slaughtered. It's a fun book to browse from start to finish, and it enjoys the distinction of avoiding the cutesy artifice common to this subgenre. William, James & Co., 2013 (3rd ed.), ISBN 978-1-59028263-2.

Developmental Editing: A Handbook for Freelancers, Authors, and Publishers Scott Norton wrote this book to help developmental editors master their part in the process. Through various author, client, and project profiles, he offers interesting context into real-world literary projects. An excellent, if perhaps insider-y, take on book editing, penned by a master. Probably one of the best books I've seen that illuminates structural problems with manuscripts—and how to fix them. University of Chicago Press, 2009, ISBN 978-0-226-59515-3.

Draft No. 4: On the Writing Process Long-time *New Yorker* writer and author of more than 30 books, John McPhee is a recognized writer's writer. This book represents his master class in the craft of writing. Presented in a graceful narrative style, he approaches his subject logically, addressing structure, relationships, composition, and reference frames. Farrar, Straus and Giroux, 2017, ISBN 978-0-374-53797-5.

Dreyer's English If you set a stretch goal of reading just one "utterly correct guide to clarity and style," this book by Benjamin Dreyer—the copy chief at Random House—makes an excellent candidate. It's a mix of plainly written usage advice and lists of reasonably accessible usage notes. The prose offers a bit of snap, sometimes collapsing into unnecessary sarcasm,[4] but the man's edited a lot of big-name writers. His advice makes for good reading for any writer who aspires to a Big Five contract. Random House, 2019, ISBN 978-0-8129-9570-1.

4: He says, whistling softly to himself.

English Grammar George Curme, a long-ago president of the Modern Language Association, presents a detailed yet compact overview of English grammar. It's a true textbook, filled with reference tables and terse rules—but it addresses many subtle rules that most contemporary grammar books omit entirely. I own a 1960 version (ninth printing) of the 1925 text originally published by Barnes and Noble. Hard to find, now, but if you can get your hands on it, it's worth its weight in gold. For writers of a certain age who learned the minutiae of grammar at the end of a nun's ruler, as I did, this book will bring back memories.

The Forest for the Trees Experienced editor Betsy Lerner shares rock-solid guidance for writers. It's not a craft book; rather, its a series of reflections about common barriers she's seen with emerging writers and advice about how to overcome them. For a softer look at the wisdom that editors wish their authors knew, this one's a home run. Riverhead Books, 2000, ISBN 978-1-57322857-2.

Garner's Modern English Usage If you can afford just one book about English usage, make it this one. Bryan A. Garner's massive text *begins* with a pronunciation guide and essays about the Usage Wars, before launching into more than 900 pages of dense usage entries. It wraps with a meta-glossary of grammar terms, a timeline of books about English usage, a bibliography, and an index. A big, heavy book filled with massive insight into current and historical use of the language. Oxford University Press, 2016 (4th ed.), ISBN 978-0-19-049148-2.

Many a Slip: A Dictionary of Shaky Grounds and Missed Connections Logic and rhetoric rarely intrude upon most fiction writers' plotlines, but perhaps they should. This book, by Gregory James, offers a concise compendium of logical errors and terms-of-art for rhetoricians. Language Centre at Hong Kong University, 2001, ISBN 962-7607-13-4.

Merriam-Webster's Dictionary of Allusions Some woe-is-me humanities wags argue that we're losing our sense of shared culture as higher education focuses more on what divides us than on what unites us. Whether you agree or disagree, one cannot escape noticing that allusions common in prior generations are almost incomprehensible to modern audiences. Books like this one, curated by Elizabeth Webber and Mike Feinsilber, offer a lifeline of meaning that spans the ages. Merriam-Webster, 1999, ISBN 0-87779-628-9.

On Writing: A Memoir of the Craft I've given a dozen copies of Stephen King's literary memoir away as gifts to aspiring writers. His book, a true memoir similar to Lamont's *Bird by Bird*, tells his story. It's worth reading for the inspiration and insight. And the humor. Scribner, 2000, ISBN 978-1-4391-5681-0.

The Penguin Dictionary of Symbols Boasting nearly 1,200 pages of in-depth but relatively contained entries, this book represents a great go-to source for learning about the hidden symbolism of some given object or term. Better yet, because the book is designed to be a symbol dictionary, you won't have to spend hours in the Wikipedia bunny hole trying to uncover the subtle symbology for otherwise common Internet search terms like *hyssop*, *shoulder*, and *dove*. Penguin Reference, 1996, ISBN 0-14-051254-3.

Roget's International Thesaurus I happen to own the third edition, released in 1962, but any version of this venerable classic is well worth the investment. "But," you protest, "I can find a thesaurus online for free, and Word features one built in!" Yes. But the benefit of a printed thesaurus—besides its availability when the Wi-Fi conks out—is that if you pick up an older version, you'll find suggestions more rich and more rare than what surface on the superficial, business-focused thesauruses attached to search engines and office applications.

Self-Publisher's Legal Handbook Helen Sedwick, a business attorney, offers "an updated guide to protecting your rights and wallet." The second edition, released in 2017, covers copyrights, privacy, pen names, printing, hiring freelancers, business structures, financing, taxes, marketing, distribution, scams, estate planning, and related subjects. A lot of ground gets covered in a short amount of easily readable space. This book is a critical resource for all authors, self-published or not. Ten Gallon Press, 2017, ISBN 978-0988302198.

Slang and Euphemism The third edition of this book, presenting itself as a dictionary of "oaths, curses, insults, ethnic slurs, sexual slang, drug talk, college lingo and related matters" is by now a bit dated, but as a reference for period vernacular, it's still quite useful. Signet Reference, 2001, ISBN 0-451-20371-2.

Storycraft: The Complete Guide to Writing Narrative Nonfiction All writing can prove powerful but well-crafted nonfiction occupies a class all of its own—a point that Jack Hart ably demonstrates. In 14 chapters covering elements of the craft (structure, point of view, action, theme, ethics, etc.) he dives into the elements of a story that make it shine. The focus is on substantive journalism, but the advice he offers and the in-depth examples he shares make this book valuable for all writers. University of Chicago Press, 2011, ISBN 978-0-226-31814-1.

The Subversive Copy Editor Professional editors work with a diversity of authors, spanning many different personality types and levels of experience. For that matter, editors themselves present many different personality types and levels of experience. Carol Fisher Saller's book serves as both insight into the daily life of an editor as well as a master text in preserving relationships among competing literary stakeholders. University of Chicago Press, 2016 (2nd ed.), ISBN 978-0-226-24007-7.

Webster's New World College Dictionary Every writer needs a dictionary. If a word isn't in your dictionary, it doesn't exist. The Associated Press relies on Webster's New World College Dictionary (fifth edition) as its authoritative reference text, and because Diction Dude adopts most of AP Style, we use WNWCD as our authoritative dictionary, too. Although you'll undoubtedly obtain free access many online dictionaries—some of which are not of good repute!—sticking with a single authoritative printed dictionary instead of whatever surfaces on Google or Bing will protect the integrity of your personal writing style. Webster's New World, 2016, ISBN 978-0-54459822-5.

What Editors Do: Art, Craft, and Business of Book Editing An anthology of short essays by experienced book editors, this collection (edited by Peter Ginna) of more than two dozen essays breaks into five sections. The first addresses editorial acquisitions—the process of finding a manuscript worth publishing. The second covers editing. The third covers marketing. The last two switch to a topical focus. Part 4 considers genres and case studies, while Part 5 looks at publishing as a career. Good material. The book speaks more to editors and aspiring editors, but the industry acumen pervading the essays proves salutary for writers, too. The University of Chicago Press, 2017, ISBN 978-0-226-29997-6.

The Wordsworth Dictionary of Phrase and Fable Although it's a bit dated now, this 1,200-page book is still a goldmine of references to myths, folk tales, literary allusions, and common legends. Quite a lot is stuffed in here. It's good for obscure references, and terms of particular utility include common idioms derived from those obscure references. Wordsworth, 1993, ISBN 978-1-85326300-2.

Writing Tools: 50 Essential Strategies for Every Writer Roy Peter Clark's book is worth reading cover to cover. He outlines 50 maxims for writing broken into four parts: "Nuts and Bolts," "Special Effects," "Blueprints," and "Useful Habits." The prose is accessible and each fairly short chapter contains copious examples to illustrate Clark's points. Little, Brown & Co., 2006, ISBN 978-0-316-01498-4.

6.3 A Note About Reading

Did you catch what's missing from the list?

Paint-By-Numbers Writing

Think twice before buying or reading books that offer templated or paint-by-numbers approaches to writing long-form fiction. This class of book emphasizes bad behavior—and often, these books are part of a slick ecosystem of products and services eager to generate additional revenue for the author while offering little of meaningful value.

When you evaluate a potential new title for your personal reference library, explore the premise of the book. If it presumes to break writing into fixed steps or chunks—presented in the form of a *method* or a *grid* or a *template*—what it's really doing is offering a block-level composition strategy. Which is a fancy way of saying that it treats writing like a baking recipe: "Add this much plot, stir in this much characterization, season with any two of these archetypes, bake for 65,000 words, then frost with inflection points at these ratios of wordcount."

The message of these method-focused books is clear: If only you paint by the numbers, you too can be a successful author.

But writing isn't a template. It's not a story grid. There's no One True Method™for designing story blocks and positioning them in a scientifically proven manner. These approaches remove the art, asking aspiring authors to engage in mere mimicry. You can teach someone how to follow a recipe but mere conformance saps the vitality and the creativity from the final product. Master literary theory—not a checklist—to understand "the recipe" with enough depth to know when to follow it and when to ignore it. There's no shortcut to success. Not even when you paint by numbers.

Writing Inspiration

Some authors find real value in books that share inspirational stories and offer motivation through writing prompts, success tips, cute anecdotes, and upbeat sloganeering.[5]

5: I am not one of those authors.

The catch with writing-inspiration books—they're often penned by the former mid-listers we discussed in the first chapter—is that they lack substance. The craft advice proves too generic to be useful and the relentlessly optimistic tone and style mislead inexperienced writers about the long, hard road that lies ahead. This "I did it and you can too" message obscures more than it illuminates.

As preparation for this book, I reviewed a dozen of these texts over a long afternoon at a Barnes & Noble café, armed with my notepad and several mugs of mocha. I ultimately couldn't recommend a single one, despite their prominent placement on the shelf and their strong sales history. The biggest reason my book-resource list lacks titles focused primarily on inspiration is because I think that even though the authors mean well, these books are either generic fluff at best, or inadvertently toxic at worst.

Read to Succeed

A bit of generalized writing advice seems to get lost in the ether: To be a world-class writer, you must be a world-class reader.

Four bits of advice on that front.

First, *read your genre*. You should be conversant with the authors and the bestsellers in your genre, including the classics. You should know (and read) the modern chart-toppers as well as the critically acclaimed or award-winning books. This engagement isn't optional. If you're not reading at least one book in your genre each month, you're falling behind. And even that's an awfully light load. Bonus points for knowing your genre's authors from your home community.

Second, *read other genres*. People who focus like a laser on what they enjoy often overlook good techniques and stories in other genres. A lot of fantasy and sci-fi writers, in particular, settle into their favorites and rarely stray from them. The value of a well-rounded reading plate—even if you rotate something different just once every fourth or fifth book—is that you get a better sense of the language and deeper exposure to other storylines and archetypes. Engage with some of the classics as well as an occasional hoity-toity award winner. Consider it research, if you must, but it's an important part of fleshing out your breadth as a writer.

Third, *study science that's relevant to your writing interests*. For example, people who delight in creating complex new worlds will profit from reading some accessible general-knowledge texts about cosmology, biology, physics, or chemistry. Developing a magic system from scratch that passes the plausibility test proves much easier when you know a little something about Newtonian physics and general relativity, particularly the equations

$$F = ma$$

and

$$E = mc^2$$

that most people studied in high school. Likewise, let your heroic wizard cast magical healing spells that work *with* biology instead of pretending that biology as a science doesn't exist.

And if you enjoy romance? Read about the science of attraction. Murder mysteries? Grab an introductory forensics textbook. Men's adventure? Take a survivalist course.

Fourth, *study a bit of critical reasoning, ethical theory, and evolutionary psychology*. Compelling conflict starts with nailing the why-and-how of a person's activities after some initial stress or obstacle. Understanding subjects like moral theory, behavioral economics, and evolutionary psychology—even at the level of having read a single introductory book on each subject—puts you head and shoulders above people whose conflict isn't rooted in any organized system of thought at all. Characters act in complex ways, but those actions must still ring true to an editor. Your odds of crossing that hurdle increase significantly if your character development is informed by a deep understanding of how people's minds work in the real world.

Advancing Your Craft

50 Informed Suggestions for Writing for Publication

7

Most writing advice proves hollow because it appears in the form of a high-level directive untethered to a specific writing goal. Instead of tinkering with generic writing rules, get started with your writing by considering some more substantive craft-focused ideas about writing for publication.

7.1 Rules?

In a June 2018 post on his *terribleminds* blog, author Chuck Wendig explored common writing-advice slogans. He urinated on them with gasoline then struck a match to the whole sopping mess. He wrote:

> Writing advice, as I am fond of saying, is bullshit. But bullshit fertilizes. It has function, if you want it to. These most common pieces of writing advice are useful for newer writers, but never good to keep as gospel, because for every piece of ironclad writing advice are ten writers who can snap that iron bar with their bare hands, breaking those rules left and right—with grace, aplomb, awards, and sales. None of this stuff is as simple as it seems on the surface, and demands a deeper scrutiny than just accepting them at shallow face-value. Dig deep. Challenge these ideas.[18]

Wendig's "frack 'em if they want to give you a rule" philosophy serves as useful counterpoint to Don McNair's "rules of fog-free writing" encapsulated in his 2013 book, *Editor-Proof Your Writing: 21 Steps to the Clear Prose Publishers and Agents Crave*. McNair offers rules. Twenty-one of them, 19 of which are pretty darn solid. And they're *rules*, so you know you have to obey them if you wish to satisfy the craving of publishers and agents.

I'm inclined to side with Wendig, though: Most writing advice is directionally useful for the inexperienced but otherwise less helpful than it seems when you try to unpack it. Good writing rarely distils to a set of bumper-sticker slogans. These craft rules—these bumper-sticker slogans of good writing—fail for two reasons.

First, every writing rule simple enough to dispense on a fortune cookie is too simple to be useful when you try to apply it to a particular problem. That's essentially Wendig's point. For a brand-new writer, these rules appear useful. As the writer matures, the emptiness of the rule becomes manifest. A great example relates to the command to "write what you know."

Since no one has left Earth, a bunch of sci-fi is now off the table. Since no one lives in the past, all historical fiction is off the table. Since no one casts spells, fantasy is off the table. Right? After all, no one *knows* first-hand about interstellar space travel or antiquity or magic, so no one's competent to write about them.

When people say "write what you know," what they *really* mean is "don't engage in cultural appropriation." Which, fine. But then you dive right into a second-order question about author agency in a fictional context, and then the conversation descends into the Chasm of High Theory. It turns out, "write what you know" isn't craft advice at all, but rather an ethical principle that, regardless of its relative virtue, isn't universally honored or even clearly defined.

The second reason these rules fail relates to their misalignment to an author's goals. Often, the rule sources from a specific perspective that isn't applicable across all genres and lengths. For example, that old chestnut to "show don't tell" might make sense in a novel. But in a flash story, the equation changes. And in a hardboiled detective story, you often get a denouement that's basically a Sherlock Holmes-style recitation of all the clues the reader missed in the preceding pages. Lots of telling, there. Sometimes, telling makes more sense than showing. Context matters.

I'd take it a step further than Wendig. I think most maxim-based writing advice is effectively useless, because it's untethered to a specific goal and often isn't geared toward writing *for publication*. High-level platitudes presented as rules or even as authoritative best practices either lead people astray or offer nothing but an empty slogan. The conceptual meat-and-potatoes behind the bumper-sticker mantra is what matters, not the slogan, yet too often that essential context is stripped, leaving a pithy phrase ideal for inspirational T-shirts and NaNoWriMo stickers but little else.

So let me strike a balance by offering 50 "informed suggestions"—not rules!—that, if internalized in your writing of fiction, will likely reduce the number of reasons an editor or an agent may reject your work outright. They're presented in the order I developed them, based on a notebook I've maintained for nearly a decade wherein I chronicled frequent challenges and their respective fixes. Significantly, you see not just the suggestion but the narrative behind it. The informed suggestions aren't merely maxims, but rather articulated principles that you may evaluate for inclusion into your own craft toolkit.

But *caveat emptor*. You're about to dive into my hobbyhorse list, and you should absolutely interpret it as such. Every editor carries his or her own similar list in a mental filing cabinet. Mine is based on the things I kept encountering in the wild, so it's got the benefit of being a list of things that drove me to distraction in the real world instead of being a list of hypothetical things I curated from other people's lists of things that drive *them* to distraction.

In other words, these suggestions aim to fix problems I see routinely. Some of them may resonate with you. Some likely won't.

7.2 The Suggestions

As a high-level summary of the craft-and-mindset of writing, I think this list offers useful advice. If you take it, you'll be better off—but I don't pretend to offer a list of "50 rules of fog-free writing" you must honor or else.

What Lies Ahead

This volume, by design, doesn't focus on the nuts-and-bolts of grammar, syntax, or style. Those subjects are covered in much greater depth in *The Diction Dude Guide to the Mechanics of Fiction*. However, the craft-heavy points that follow offer a good first glimpse of my high-level approach to mechanics. I share them to offer you at least a little bit of craft stuff to get you started on your journey as a professional writer.

1. Start with the end in mind. Whether you plan a story in minute detail or let 'er fly and see where the story takes you, you probably ought to know how the story will end—even if you don't know the path it'll take to get there. Experienced editors encounter quite a few stories that start fun, then begin to bloat a bit, then suddenly everything kinda-sorta resolves in a quasi-satisfying finish when the author realized he ran out of word count.

Stories that end because the author called it a day, versus stories that end because the plot and conflict culminated in a well-paced denouement, read very differently. Especially in the final 20 percent of the book.

2. Show, don't tell—unless telling makes more sense. The slogan "show, don't tell" gets drilled into workshop participants, and the dictum can be extended to the point of purple-prose ridiculousness, but the concept is sound: It's often better to reveal something happening than to simply assert that it did, and it's more respectful to the reader to hint or imply behaviors instead of definitively ascribing emotions.[1]

For example, you could write something like: "Bob, a fat old man who rarely bathed, sat on the bus." But it's better to write something like: "As Bob sprawled into a seat-and-a-half on the bus, he reached for the handrail to steady himself. Sally wrinkled her nose at the sour stench wafting from the elderly man's now-open, sweat-stained armpit." Just don't get so involved that the prose turns purple, though—as with much related to literary styling, virtue lies amidst the shades of grey.

In almost no case is it useful to "tell" the story of the mechanics or backstory of a fictional universe. Those nuggets of information, useful as they may be to the reader, are best demonstrated rather than data-dumped in narration. The caveat, of course, is that sometimes delivering a bit of exposition offers a more succinct approach to informing the reader than belaboring the point through tangential action or dialogue—think, for example, of most Michael Crichton novels. No two authors will agree on the dividing line between showing and telling; nevertheless, most editors eager to reject a *novice* writer's story during a slush-pile vetting will not look favorably upon vast seas of exposition. The grace to tell, not show, often tends to accrue more to established writers than to emerging ones.

1: *Purple prose* is the generic term for language littered with superfluous adverbs, syntactical complexity, and precocious diction. Consider this infamous description of a cocktail: "Once in the hands of Duncan Nicol it was translated, as by consecration in the name of a divinity more benevolent than all others, into pisco punch, the wonder and glory of San Francisco's heady youth, the balm and solace of fevered generations, a drink so endearing and inspired that although its prototype has vanished, its legend lingers on, one with the Grail, the unicorn, and the music of the spheres." (Lucius Beebe, *Gourmet* magazine, 1957.)[19]

3. Embrace the reader as a co-creator of your universe. The best stories invite the reader to play along in her own mind. As such, over-prescribing the content—through too much concrete description or mental narration, mostly—deprives the reader the chance to participate in your creative endeavor.

You need not affix every detail in an attempt to clarify "authorial intent" or to develop a "unique voice." Be vague, sometimes. Let the reader figure things out on her own. When you hint and suggest, you allow for a richer diversity of emotional engagement than when you assert facts definitively.

For example, instead of asserting that an old woman sitting in a chair is sad, describe her as sitting slumped in her chair and absently stroking a dog-curled photograph while staring impassively into the sunset. We readers know that she's sad but we can also infer wistfulness or melancholy or denial in the stroking and staring. However, when we're *told* she's sad, that's it. One emotion, definitively proscribed by the author, and we're not allowed to draw any other conclusion. How depressing for a reader!

Authors plant seeds in the minds of their readers; the readers water those seeds and let their own little gardens bloom. Respect the co-generative nature of that garden, and the reader will remain loyal. If you dictate the shape and size and smell of each flower—well, why should the reader bother entering the garden only to discover that there's no opportunity to tend it with you?

4. Villains aren't always ugly. Heroes aren't always beautiful. A novice writer reveals herself through heroic main characters who are perfect in every way; those beautiful heroes are opposed by villains who are very obviously physically or emotionally deformed.

Some of the most beautiful people in the world can be villains (see Justin Bieber, in his badboy phase circa 2013) and the most humdrum can be saints (see: St. Theresa of Calcutta). Virtue and vice are not correlated with beauty or emotional stability. Unless you're writing an allegory, this kind of stereotyping generally fails to earn loyal readers.

The point works in reverse, too: a plain, ordinary hero against powerful, beautiful adversaries is similarly trite.

5. Beware the too-tidy ending. Wrapping a story so that all the bad guys earn their punishment and all the heroes bask in glory—with no plot strings left untied!—usually proves problematic, because so much *stuff* has to happen at the end that the author ends up muddling the denouement just to sprinkle pixie dust on the fairy tale.

Let things be messy. Let the bad guys eke at least a partial victory. Let the heroes suffer despite their triumph. Conflict implies change, after all. Black-and-white storytelling rarely proves compelling in anything other than children's books.

6. Read your archive. Instead of deleting your old material and misguided drafts, save all of it. Then, every so often, pull those notes and deleted scenes from the file drawer and read them. You may be surprised to see how you've grown—or how you've backslid.

Deletion is for the cowardly.

7. Write with cats and martinis. Write in a setting comfortable to you, with the requisite accoutrements that facilitate productive writing. Each person's list differs. I do my best writing late at night, supported by an amber-on-black full-screen display and a beeswax pillar candle—it must be pure beeswax, none of that soy garbage!—and a martini and Fiona d'Cat sleeping between my mechanical keyboard and the monitor. In the summer, I keep the window open and let the West Michigan night air and the gentle sounds of downtown life provide a soothing acoustic backdrop; in the winter, I light a roaring wood fire in my office fireplace and wrap myself in a plush terrycloth robe.

The point is, writing isn't an exercise in apart-ism. You need not build yourself a special writing jail on the theory that it will "make" you more productive. It won't. What aids productivity is comfort and focus. Aspiring writers often obsess over their writing environment to the detriment of actually writing.

For me, it's cats and martinis. For you, it's likely something else. Pick what works for you and recognize that over-analyzing and incessantly tweaking your writing space adversely affects your writing productivity.

8. One perfect word is better than a litany of pedestrian phrases. It's not true that all words and sentences must be comprehensible to a fourth grader—unless you're writing for a fourth-grade audience. There's a difference between writing in a highly formal and stilted fashion, versus writing so ploddingly that the beauty and the majesty of the language withers in desuetude, versus writing in a crisp yet spare style that makes the story shine. Pick the right word for the setting and the sentence, even if the word is relatively uncommon. You're allowed to use rare words provided you do it infrequently enough to avoid sounding pedantic to your book's target market.

That last point governs: If you write literary fiction published by university presses, your indulgence of the sesquipedalian accrues more grace than if you're writing middle-grade fantasy stories through a Big Five imprint.

9. "Just Say No" to rape as a plot device. Rape is serious; it's not a cheap ploy you can trot out when you write yourself into a plot hole. Also: People don't magically "get over" having been raped in the next chapter. Also also: Women don't later learn to understand and forgive their rapists as being aggressive, manly, virtuous men who were merely misunderstood. Also also also: Men can be raped, too.

Although most writers now avoid casual racism, it's astonishing to still see writers—including female genre writers—deploy careless rape tropes. There's nothing funny or magical or plot-enhancing about sexual assault. However, an author who introduces sexual assault in a sensitive way, after careful research, with purpose, can bring power to a story. If you write about rape, make it matter and do your homework.

Know What You Write

Volunteer for 20 hours at a rape-crisis center before you write about rape, if you've never been sexually assaulted. Then consider whether you really ought to include this plot point.

The suggestion holds for other things, too—for example, an upper-middle-class writer who yearns to write about homelessness should volunteer at a soup kitchen for 20 hours first. If you can engage with difficult subjects before you write about them, then doing so leads to more powerful and more authentic storytelling.

10. Deploy the Five Whys. People experienced with industrial quality-control principles enjoy a "tool" called the *Five Whys*. The principle is simple: For every problem statement, ask why. For each answer, ask why again. And repeat through five iterations. The point isn't to act like a precocious toddler; rather, the point is to arrive at a clear-eyed understanding of root causes.

Something like a Five Whys exercise makes a lot of sense for story writers, too. Every time you reach an inflection point in the story, ask why the inflection point makes more sense than any plausible alternative. Do your answers track cleanly back to Page One? Similarly, when a character makes a choice or a plot-critical event transpires, ask why that choice even matters, and why it must be *this* rather than *that*.

A good Five Whys opportunity lies within stories that feature several borderline-plausible pivots. I've encountered very many stories over the years in which the author inserted some *deus ex machina* moment or a character makes an out-of-character choice.[2] And then another. And then another. And by the end of the story, the whole setup seems forced or even absurd—but the author, because he penned a "plot-driven story," didn't see the forest through the plot-twist trees.

2: In the real world, people sometimes act out of character. In a fictional world, a character who acts out-of-character hasn't been adequately characterized by the author.

As an author, the *why* question is the most powerful weapon in your crafting toolkit. Use it ruthlessly.

11. Drink deeply from your own well before appropriating others' experiences. Your life is too rich, too precious, to ignore it as a source of inspiration. Write with your heart and your mind; avoid trying to inflame the hearts of others through mindless prose devoid of experiential nuance.

That said, working in fiction often requires you to write what you don't know. Every person who creates a new fictional universe makes it up, after all. But that's not the point. The sundry tensions of the human experience speak most effectively with the subtle, seasoned voice of writers who've previously experienced them. You're welcome to fake it, or to apply your own experiences in creative ways, but editors and increasingly readers deploy a zero-tolerance approach to perceived appropriation narratives. In fact, some larger presses hire people who specifically search manuscripts for red flags of cultural appropriation. They're called *sensitivity readers* and they've been hired to predict potential reader outrage in an era of #OwnVoices advocacy and the overwhelmingly toxic Twitter cancel culture.

You're an interesting person. Use what you've been given; your inheritance is more generous than you think.

12. Strong writers develop strong plots; weak writers develop plot twists. Twists work well and are even welcome in certain genres like horror, mystery, and suspense, but in most other genres, if you have to twist then you didn't plot it right in the first place. Readers will suspend disbelief if they're in the garden with you, helping to cultivate the story suggested by the words on your page. An inappropriate or poorly executed twist changes the biology of the garden, knocking the reader's expectation of the story off-kilter.

If you can't write your way out of a plot hole, blow up the story and start over. Beware the impulse to save bad plotting with an equally bad or implausible plot twist.

13. People rarely do big things for just one reason. Avoid suggesting that characters have just *one* all-encompassing, obvious, well-understood, and transparent reason for doing big, important things. The ocean of motivation is filled from a thousand different streams of intention and values. The exploration of a tributary or two often leads to fruitful sharpening of conflict or enrichment of plot arcs.

For example, in the *Wheel of Time* series by Robert Jordan—finished after Jordan's death by Brandon Sanderson—the character Galadedrid Damodred is notable for being motivated exclusively by a duty-bound sense of right and wrong. And Jordan plays up this monochromatic motivation frequently, contrasting Galad with his more-chill half-brother Gawyn Trakand. Galad works because he's the only member of that vast cast of characters who acts with such perfect rectitude. But he also works because he's only a mid-tier character who appears often but isn't a primary POV character.

Unless you're writing the next Galad, remember that your characters should do things for several and inconsistent reasons that aren't predictable from just one or two data points. Real-life is messy. Fictional life should be, too.

14. You probably shouldn't discover your characters as you write them. I hear writers say things like, "By the time I got to the middle of the story, I learned that my character likes cheddar cheese." Bollocks! If you don't know a character until the middle of the story, then what the heck was the character doing at the beginning of the story? Clearly, the beginning of the story requires a 100-percent rewrite—now that you know your characters.

Some people who plan minimally before they write enjoy discovering the personality of characters through the drafting process. That writing process is certainly valid. However, you may find it valuable to write independent short character sketches for these characters to introduce them to yourself before you incorporate them into a more substantive work of fiction. Not only can you deploy these sketches on your website (a value-add for your fans!), but you'll likely save a ton of time rewriting your early material to conform to the characters as they flourished only after you finally understood them.

15. Ellipses are a tool of Satan. Ellipses remain, of course, a valid form of punctuation. But used too often—i.e., more than once every 10,000 words or so—they strongly signify over-prescription. You don't need to explicitly tell the reader about every pause or trail-off a character experiences in dialogue. The reader's co-created mental garden will tend to that trail-off—and even if the reader doesn't, it's not important enough of a detail to belabor. If the trail-off is absolutely relevant to the plot, *and it probably isn't,* indicate it with narration instead of through punctuation.

People think I'm joking when I say this, but I'm not: When I peruse a new submission, I skim the whole document before I start reading. If I see too many ellipses, I don't even bother reading the first sentence.[3] It's an automatic rejection because the author is telegraphing to me that he or she isn't skilled enough to overcome the amateur's tendency to over-prescribe the dialogue within a scene.

3: It's not at all unusual to encounter new-author manuscripts with ellipses appearing as frequently as once every 500 words—or, on average, once every other page.

Editors Are People Too

Every editor stables a hobbyhorse or three that you cannot predict and which probably isn't even fair. Mine happens to be ellipses, and I'm the first to admit that my hatred of those three little dots borders on the absurd. Nevertheless, I persist.

Generally speaking, a conservative approach to the language reduces your risk that a curmudgeonly editor will mount some ignoble syntactical steed then beat it into shoe leather before dismounting and then rejecting your submission. Editors are people too, and we aren't always rational. A colleague of mine, for example, spikes stories presented using a sans-serif typeface because "it's too hard to read." Another feels very strongly against starting a story with dialogue, for reasons that baffle me.

16. Beware long stories with a single point-of-view character. The longer the story, the more value you'll obtain from introducing several characters who enjoy point-of-view privilege. Here's why:

1. Long stories told from one person's perspective grow tiring to read, particularly if that character evidences some tic like reflexive sarcasm or self-doubt that proves tolerable only in small doses.
2. Readers can't fully humanize any given point-of-view character except through the eyes of other point-of-view characters, any more than you can fully flesh out yourself by staring into a mirror. Thus, your POV character never really becomes three-dimensional to your readers, despite that this character mediates the entire story.
3. Using just one POV character severely circumscribes the author's flexibility to incorporate subplots that involve other characters.

4. Single-POV stories often require "coffee-shop scenes" wherein other characters bring the POV character up-to-speed on something critical to the story—not for the character's benefit, but for the readers' background knowledge. It's implausible in one story with several characters that the POV character knows everything salient to the story from the narrator's 50,000-foot perspective, but that's the framework that a single-POV story enforces.
5. Single-POV stories are especially amenable to info dumps by the narrator that assert private facts about other characters for the sake of contextualizing the POV character's thoughts or actions.

My wholly unscientific and heavily caveated suggestion: Add a primary POV character for every 20,000 words of manuscript.

17. Remember thy cloud drive and keep it synced. No excuse justifies losing your work. Keep your stuff on your hard drive (don't bother with flash drives) and keep that folder synced to the cloud using Google Drive, Microsoft OneDrive, Dropbox, Box, OwnCloud, GitLab, or whatever service you prefer. Local copy + folder sync = bliss. Flash drives are *so* last century.

18. If your last paragraph renders all preceding paragraphs moot, you're doing it wrong. Attention flash writers: The whole "I'm going to shock you with a final sentence that completely changes the story" routine is cliché. Bait-and-switch is just as disreputable for writers as it is for advertisers. If you endure the effort to create characters and a plot and a clear arc that invites reader buy-in, let that work culminate in closure for the reader. Generally speaking, a reader wants to experience a story, not your clever attempt at rug-pulling.

19. You can't sleep with your main character. Avoid developing a main character who's basically the best-case respondent to your Tinder or Grindr or Her ad. No one's perfect, not even a hero, and sometimes the savvy reader can sense when an author has fallen in love or lust with a favored character.

Lots of experts advise against a Mary Sue character—someone who's flawless and omnicompetent, and often considered a form of author self-insertion or wish fulfillment. Readers sniff it from a mile away; this character acts as a wrecking ball on the story's plot-conflict nexus.

On the flip side, don't let the fear of Mary Sues dissuade you from writing strong female characters. After all, 50 percent of the population really is above average. The balancing act between Mary Sue and above-average heroine sometimes clarifies with a simple question: "Is [insert behavior here] plausible, both in itself and within the context of the plot as it has unfolded?" A Five Whys inquiry proves fruitful here.

(Same holds true for Marty Stu, the male version of the trope, by the way.)

20. *Said* is your best friend. No need to *declaim* or *exclaim* or *shout* or *whisper* or *suggest* or whatever. Just *say*. The word blends into the background as a train conductor, so your reader doesn't get derailed from the story by means of unfortunate synonym-hopping.

No need to be a fanatic about it; as long as *said* predominates, you're probably fine.

A few authorities—McNair jumps to mind—suggest that even *said* is unnecessary and that the character who acts immediately preceding a floating bit of dialogue should be inferred as the speaker. This approach, to my editor's eye, seems substandard and ought to be avoided, although many editors find this approach to be perfectly satisfactory. Despite that speech tags are only necessary when there's ambiguity about who's talking, the syntactical proximity of a different sentence's grammatical subject isn't sufficient to imply speakership under conventional, conservative interpretations of English syntax. Use speech tags when they're necessary to clarify the speaker or to signify a change in speakers. Do not rely on implications based on the non-verbal actors in antecedent sentences to do the work for you.[4]

4: Also: Quite a few readers skim over books as they read; they don't parse every word and sentence in detail. It's usually better to supply concrete cues than to rely on reader inferences, because those inferences aren't always shaped by a close read. Hence, err on the side of incorporating speech tags.

21. If you torture an animal in print, you might be reported to the feds. Sometimes people like to write about how they learned the nobility of nature or bonded with their father or whatnot over a weekend spent at the hunting blind. This theme is common among my submitters, particularly younger males, given our Upper Midwestern locale. And the theme, intrinsically, is fine. Then shoot the animal and give it a fitting, quick death. But to dive into excruciating detail, over several pages, about how it bleeds and moans and labors to stand and breathe—that kind of writing can be a red flag when slides into torture porn.

If we've learned nothing else from reading the blog posts and personal journals of school shooters, for example, fantasizing about causing pain to animals is a common marker of later tendencies to real-life violence.

In fact, *I encourage all editors to report to law-enforcement officials any story that glorifies the torture of an animal.* There's zero literary merit in this practice. Zero. And non-trivial evidence that the author requires psychological intervention.[5]

5: No, I'm not exaggerating for effect.

22. The more you try to sound transgressive, the more you sound like a fool. Experimental styles are difficult to pull off and typically work well only for experienced MFA-prepared authors. Many of the stream-of-consciousness styles—offering deep penetration with myriad mental asides interspersed with first-person narration and inconsistent punctuation and italics—don't come off as trendy, but rather as tedious in the hands of the inexperienced. It's difficult to read and it tends to take the reader out of the story, forcing her to be a meta-reader instead.

Master Standard English before moving on to more advanced case studies.

23. Good editors check facts. Your editor will verify universal truths about the world, so it pays to get the details correct during the drafting process. Even in an invented world, the world itself must be internally self-consistent, and a good editor will spot inconsistencies. It's usually better if those flaws don't make it to the editor in the first place.

In other words, you don't have *carte blanche* to just make things up willy-nilly. Your universe must cohere at the level of physics, chemistry, and biology—and a basic principle of coherence is the Principle of Non-Contradiction.

24. Fire Chekhov's gun. Stuff that's important at the beginning of the story should at least be addressed by the end of the story. For example, belaboring an otherwise insignificant detail like a particular character's earrings should result in those earrings being relevant to the story in some way.

It's useful to re-read a story looking for the emphasis of people, places, things, or ideas to verify that the relative prominence they receive is commensurate to their significance to the story. Sometimes, a detail that sounds fun in Chapter 2 gets lost by Chapter 5, but some readers will hit Chapter 7 wondering about that detail.

One common misfire: Using an extended description of a thing (a tattoo, an artifact, a weapon, whatever) as a plot hook to launch a character in a different direction or to segue into backstory. But unless the thing being described is relevant later in the story, using it as a hook isn't helpful.

25. A character's inner voice probably shouldn't sound like *MST3K* commentary. Contemporary fiction seems to favor first-person or close third-person points of view larded with internal dialogue barely different in tone and structure from the narration that surrounds it. The risk for the author arises when that interior dialogue starts to sound like either the author himself, or the sarcastic overdub à la *Mystery Science Theater 3000*. Even if you package them as character thoughts, no editor worth his salt will fail to notice the author intrusion inherent in the proliferation of snarky narrative asides.

The tone-discrepant inner dialogue (and it's almost always sarcasm that's the offender) often stands at stark contrast with the character's overall nature and outward demeanor given a scene's context. Inner and outer dialogue should at least cohere in terms of tone and voice. Outwardly meek adolescents, for example, rarely run a simultaneous witty interior monologue while they're being bullied on a school bus. And character voice should admit to some trait that segregates it from narration. Either different language or the use of italics usually offers adequate contextual guidance for the reader.

26. Let descriptions evolve over time. There's no need to lard 274 descriptors into a paragraph. Sometimes doling out little bits of information over time helps the reader co-create the world while minimizing the narrative disruption that attends to explicit scenery info-dumps.

27. Only masochists enjoy lectures about morals or politics. Especially in fiction, overt didacticism may prove off-putting to readers who would rather be entertained instead of harangued. Certain genres admit to didactic themes (sci-fi, in particular) but in general, think twice before using a work of *genre fiction* as a vehicle for proselytizing some moral, religious or political conviction if the point of the work as a whole isn't obviously allegorical.

Literary fiction, however, marches to a different drummer. Lit-fic stories abound with moral preening and virtue signaling of various kinds.[6]

6: Which may be why so few people outside of Creative Writing Culture actually read them.

28. Almost no one "suddenly realizes" things. Avoid the crutch of introducing some fact that a character "suddenly noticed" or "quickly remembered." This approach suffers from two flaws. First, it tends to support a poor-man's transition into unnecessary backstory, and second, it suggests some sort of perceptual schizophrenia wherein "voices" (i.e., the narrator or the author) insert data relevant mostly to the reader, in the form of memory or perception experienced by the character that a normal real-world human wouldn't find remarkable. Stuff like "Jane slipped on the rug, then she suddenly realized that her ankle had given out" or "Bob quickly remembered that three weeks ago, Sally had given him the combination to the lock" comes off, correctly, as amateurish writing.

Not only is this foible clunky, but it's a painfully obvious *deux ex* moment when the main character "suddenly remembered" something that pivots the plot to the next inflection point.

29. Journal frequently. Even though you should read your archive, you should also keep a writer's diary. Record the stuff you do. Your creative blocks. Your insights. Your ideas. Your submissions and their responses. Just as you cannot become a master scuba diver without a logbook justifying your diving history, you cannot become a master author without a journal celebrating your writing history. A writer without a journal is like a clown without a van that's filled with candy and parked down by the river: a confusing, misdirected and somewhat sinister facsimile of the real thing.

A writing journal isn't the same thing as a personal diary. Focus your journal on your craft. If you want to incorporate it into a diary, great. But the goal is to record your evolution as an author.[7]

7: Consider using your author blog as your writing journal. Especially for emerging authors, reflections about the process of writing help to attract an audience and retain reader loyalty. Plus, it answers the incessant "but what should I write about?" lament so frequently wailed by the resistant.

30. Excessive parentheticals suggest a disorganized writer. Parentheticals in blog posts or non-fiction work are one thing; adding them to fiction is a different thing altogether. People write with parentheses, but we don't speak with those marks, so interspersing them frequently in dialogue or narration suggests a rewrite opportunity.

31. Adverbs aren't your friend. Or your enemy. Slash every modifier that's not essential to the story. Draw the broad, simple outlines of the story and allow the reader supply his own baroque ornamentation. Watch especially for adverbs denoting small but indeterminate units of time (*quickly, immediately, suddenly,* etc.) because they're utterly useless.

Corollary: Some adjectives and adverbs are relevant to the story. Keep those.

The trick with adverbs is that none are too few, many are too many, but finding the golden mean vexes even the best of writers. The question for any given modifier relates to usefulness. Does it do something that's essential to the sentence in the context of the story? If it does, keep it. If it doesn't, or if you're unsure, cut it.

32. Other characters aren't what they "seem." Although it's a common foible, it's best to avoid narration that asserts what a non-POV character *seems* to be doing. If the narrator is omniscient, then the narrator can assert with authority. If the narrator is not omniscient, then it's better to rely on the thoughts or observations of the POV character instead of ascribing intent through a "seems" statement.

For example, recast: "Linda entered the room. George seemed to hear her, because he stopped whistling." The problem with this sentence is that the narrator is implying causation without asserting causation. As an alternative you could write: "George stopped whistling when Linda entered the room" (definitive causation) or "Linda entered the room; she wondered if George heard her because he stopped whistling" (character speculation).

33. No one cares about the backstory, including your characters. Authors who take great care in the creation of their fictional world often want to share their labor of love with the reader. The reader, by and large, doesn't give a damn. Many stories, including some short stories, clock in with so much up-front backstory that the plot arc twists into a pretzel shoved into the tail-end of the manuscript.

You don't need backstory. If a specific bit of information is relevant, it's not backstory *by definition* and should be interwoven in the narrative like any other fact. Avoid data dumps, including dumps "cleverly" disguised as reminiscences—because people really don't spend a lot of time discussing or thinking about specific truths about the past or the physics of the their universe, particularly when those facts ever-so-conveniently dovetail with the story about to unfold.

34. Respect the eye in the sky. The narrator—the "eye in the sky"—enjoys a specific tone and voice and background knowledge based on the story's structural point of view. Keeping POV straight can be a real challenge, especially within stories with several POV characters. The voice of your narrator must be distinct, in most cases, from the voice of the point-of-view character, so the reader may distinguish between the two. Disambiguating the POV character from the narrator in first-person or close third-person points of view often trips up early-career authors. It's worth studying POV in depth, because if you screw it up, you'll need to effect a *complete* rewrite to fix it.

35. Use double quotes and place punctuation within them. Use double quotes to set off spoken dialogue but italics without quotes to render mental dialogue. Punctuation goes inside the quotes. There is almost never a circumstance in standard fiction writing wherein a period or comma falls outside a closing quotation mark.[8]

8: Well, unless you're British.

In first-person writing, narrative and inner dialogue intersperse without problem because the narrator and the speaker are the same character. However, in third-person POVs, the voice of the narrator and the inner voice of the POV character ought to be distinct. The usual method for effecting this differentiation is italics for mental speech.

36. People control their bodies. A person looks around a room; a person's eyes may be the instrument of that vision, but the eyes themselves aren't doing the looking as if they're autonomous agents in their own right. Constructs like "his eyes scanned the room" are common as a literary device but when used to excess, they suggest a sloppiness that confuses whole-vs-part agency. Body parts generally function under the jurisdiction of a person and rarely act of their own volition. Similarly, in fantasy or sci-fi action scenes, you see a lot of weapons serving as the subjects of sentences even though those things aren't really the actors. Swords clang, shields clash, wands spew fire, spears fly, guns shoot, lasers zap—but shouldn't the focus be on the people wielding those tools, rather than the tools themselves?

You get a small number of passes on the agency question before the reader rightfully questions the quality of the composition. It's true that metonymy is a valid literary device, but there's a difference between metonymy and misplaced agency that editors watch for. In particular, beware storytelling that reads as if it's really just the collected subtitles of the feature-film version of the novel.

37. Plots are driven by conflict, not by events. Many a syntactically well-written story has been rejected because the plot consisted of one damned thing after another—a sequence of events—that might have been tied together by circumstance, yet that circumstance wasn't fueled by conflict.

Conflict drives plot, not the other way around. If you cannot articulate what your protagonist wants, what's stopping him from getting it, and the path by which he overcomes the obstacles to achieve his goal, you don't have a clear conflict. It's generally wise to plan your conflict before you set a scene-by-scene structure to the story, to ensure that there's a clear reason why event A transitions to event B and then to event C.

Plot-Driven Stories

What about a "plot-driven story?" Some writers downplay or ignore conflict in the same way that a summer blockbuster action film downplays nuance. A lot of men's-adventure stories follow this path; the conflict is no more deep than "the hero beds the girl and defeats the bad guy."

The term *plot-driven story* frequently raises red flags with editors and agents. It's telegraphing a story that's likely to engender hard-to-fix structural defects in pacing and plausibility.

Even the literary equivalent of a *Transformers* movie profits from well-developed conflict. Don't fool yourself into thinking otherwise.

38. Juxtaposition stories are hard to follow. A common structural approach in fiction entails rapid switches between times, places, or characters. Often, this switching occurs at a sub-scene level, meaning that apart from a line break, the content jumps chaotically, like one of them there flying Quidditch thingies.

Juxtaposing content in this fashion isn't bad, but it's also hard to pull off. Use it only when there's a real value to let the reader see in quasi-real-time how two different aspects of the story unfold in parallel. Using it to weave two lightly related stories into a single narrative is more a literary-fiction convention than a genre-fiction convention.

39. Strange names alienate readers. The desire to invent complex names that defy English pronunciation standards isn't a sign of sublime creativity—it's a sign of amateurism.

The grid of which letters can be successfully combined in English isn't infinitely extensible—in fact, *phonics* is the study of which character combinations offer meaning within a given language. Violate English phonics rules, and readers are left unsure about how a name ought to be pronounced. They therefore disengage from the story. Don't delude yourself into thinking that your invented language must have invented names that don't sound like English—it's a trick every editor has seen, and rejected, umpteen thousands of times.

It's okay to sometimes include characters named *Bob* or *Jane* instead of *D'Qfish'znothk* or *hyedZrexxitesx*.

Likewise, resist the temptation to offer creative misspellings of common names simply to make them appear exotic. *Lidia* is usually preferable to *Laediyah*, for example.[9]

9: No editor is fooled by these shenanigans.

40. When in doubt, be consistent. Whatever physics govern your universe, those rules must apply consistently within the story. Especially in fantasy or magic-laden stories, readers will gleefully suspend disbelief about the physics of your world, but when those physics are open to inconsistent application to address plot glitches, readers notice.

Whatever you do, do consistently.

Be especially alert for "special powers" in a quasi-realistic world. For example, it's okay to introduce a system of magic, but it's more difficult to create several separate and disjoined physics to govern different aspects of a magical universe. A fantasy world where people can channel secret powers is one thing; incorporating in that same world a completely different "magic" that allows characters to fluently speak any possible language is quite another. The use of magical energy cannot provide characters with mental facilities not related to the source of that magic or to give them knowledge that they do not already possess. A good editor will catch these discrepant systems of magic and push back against them.

Put differently: Even when you make it up, you're still on the hook for inventing a system of magic that doesn't overtly contradict the laws of physics, biology, chemistry and mathematics—yet remains internally coherent.[10]

10: Your universe gets one, and only one, system of magic. A suggestion that your universe supports many competing forms of magic, each with its own physics and logic model, doesn't hold water—because each of those magics must cohere with a base physics that governs the world as a whole. It's okay to have one magic system with different expressions, but not many magic systems whose rules contradict each other and the universe within which they're situated.

41. Write your story instead of its Cliff's Notes abridgment. Particularly in short fiction, some authors are so eager to stuff a novel's worth of content into a novelette that the end result is a glorified story synopsis instead of a real story. *Slow down.* Write your stories and let them flow as long or short as necessary.

42. Verb with authority. Favor active verbs. You're certainly welcome to use passive-voice constructions on occasion, but watch for relative ratios. Stories with proliferating passive constructions tend to be flabbier and less engaging.

Watch, too, for infinitives, participles, and gerunds. They're legitimate parts of speech, but they're often deployed by weak writers as a substitute for a specific, well-chosen, active-voice main verb. Instead of writing, "Walking through the park, Melanie decided to watch as the kids were playing soccer"—write instead, "Melanie watched the kids' soccer game while she walked through the park."

Progressive-Aspect Verbs

It's rarely necessary to write in progressive aspect. For example, a present perfective sentence is: "Jane walks to the store." The present progressive is "Jane is walking to the store." Use progressive aspect only when it's necessary to indicate *ongoing* action. Many writers default to "is/was X-ing" verb forms incorrectly, sapping the literary strength from the sentence.

43. Remove your writing prompts. Writing prompts offer a fun way to get out of a temporary rut or to meet a challenge in a group-writing setting. But some prompts are silly or contrived. When the prompt has served its purpose, remove it from the manuscript.

44. Resist redundancies. A great self-edit strategy includes hunting for redundancies. Look for phrases, including common idioms, that either duplicate words or which present tautologies. For example, don't write, "He watched her with his eyes." Surely, he's not watching her with his nostrils! Likewise, think twice about expressions like "without rhyme or reason" outside of deliberately colloquial dialogue.

More insidious are the redundancies that aren't tautologies but rather a litany of steps leading to a desired final action—i.e., stage directions. For example, "She reached out her hand to clasp his" is better rendered as "She clasped his hand." Why? Because you cannot clasp someone else's hand without first extending your own. Likewise, "Mark picked up the phone and dialed the number to reach Bridget" is better as "Mark called Bridget." And "Henrietta pulled out the chair to sit down" is better as "Henrietta sat on the chair." It's rarely necessary to list the constituent sub-actions a character performs to do something, particularly when that something is utterly mundane. What matters is the sitting or the calling or the clasping, not the intermediate steps it takes to do so.

45. Avoid filtering facts and action through a character's experience or perception. Beware the dreaded *character filter*—a writing foible that inserts extra perceptual frames separating the reader from the action of the story. Filtered prose forces the action to relay through a character rather than through narration.

Consider this example:[20]

> Mary *felt* a sinking feeling as she sped across the room to yank aside the curtains. She *wondered* if her husband would really leave. She *saw* him throw the suitcase into the car and slam the door. He *seemed* angry as his gaze met hers. He pointed a finger, dropping his thumb like a gun. Now she *knew* he would go and not return. She *decided* to beg and ran outside, sinking to her knees on the cold cement. The car's tires spun, and she *felt* the gravel spitting at her as she *saw* the vehicle careen onto the road.

Get rid of those italicized filters. Isn't this better?

> Mary's stomach sank as she sped across the room to yank aside the curtains. Would her husband truly go? Bill threw the suitcase into the car and slammed the door. He turned. Her gaze met his, and his eyes narrowed. He pointed a finger, dropping his thumb like a gun. A cold chill enveloped her; he would leave and not return. She ran outside, sinking to her knees on the cold cement. The car's tires spun, spitting gravel at her as the vehicle careened onto the road.

Filtering is harder to avoid when you write first-person or close third-person stories. It's also really, really easy to engineer paragraph-length data dumps filled with this kind of writing. As a rule, if you can relay an action directly, do so; don't relay it through the additional layer of what the character thought or felt.[11]

11: Filtering is especially common with writers who allow the narrator to assert the character's thoughts and feelings instead of letting the character show them directly. It relates to the show-don't-tell conversation.

46. Watch for ESL prose. A shift of pedagogy two generations ago left many native English students reliant on the patterns and practices of English that approximate English as a Second Language education. Modern English instruction increasingly entails the use of a fairly limited vocabulary, with a resultant reliance on passive-voice sentences and auxiliary constructions (prepositional phrases, infinitive phrases) to flesh out meaning in lieu of a precise but uncommon active-voice verb.

For example, modern English students might write: "The prime minister was killed by militants by being pushed out of a window of a high-rise building." But that idea is better presented as: "Militants defenestrated the prime minister." Yes, some readers may retire to a dictionary. All the better.

Never use five words when one will suffice. Therefore, avoid relying on verbs in the form of *to be* or *to have*—they're intrinsically weak. For example, instead of the weak sentence "He had a stomach ache," it's better to write, "His stomach ached." Most verbs in the is/have universe may be simply deleted, with the logical object of those verbs taking over as the new main verb.

As a creative-writing exercise, select a short story or sample chapter of yours and highlight every one-syllable verb. How many of those sentences could be tightened if you replaced the one-syllable verb and its supporting adverbs and prepositional phrases with a single, more robust polysyllabic verb?[12]

12: I'm a fan of the idea of a *concepts-to-syllables ratio*. The more syllables you deploy to express a single idea, the flabbier the writing.

47. Read your work aloud, sometimes in public. If you aspire to commercial publication, you'll have to read in public at some point. May as well learn the skill early, especially if you're nervous about it.

Better yet: Record your readings, whether public or private. You'll pick up on verbal glitches in your writing as well as visual glitches in your reading by experiencing the text and its presentation in a different light.

48. Hook the reader by the end of the first page. I need to know what I'm in for by the end of the first page or I'm not reading further. Hooks are essential. Give the reader a reason to turn the page—or the reader won't. And an acquisitions editor certainly won't!

A good hook illuminates two things simultaneously: It tells us how the starting point of the story is different from the main character's normal life—in other words, it answers the question of *why does the book start* here *rather than somewhere else?* It also hints at the central conflict of the story by introducing the protagonist and some element of the conflict.

I don't think there are hard-and-fast, thou-shalt rules for first-page hooks. What matters is that the reader knows what's different about *now* and gets a clue about the main conflict arc. Usually, the opening of the story begins Act I, so we witness the moment where the main character's eternal yesterday transitions into the today that launches the conflict-and-plot sequence that follows. It's the "Picture it, Sicily, 1942" moment where everything changes.[13]

13: Sophia Petrillo is my spirit animal.

What rarely works well for a hook? Generally: Backstory. Lugubrious character and setting descriptions about irrelevant characters and places. Non-germane conversation. Starting with minor characters. Teed-up preludes before the action starts five pages later. Rhetorical questions. Prologues. Sarcastic mental dialogue. The narrator summarizing the mental state of the POV character. "It was a dark and stormy night."

Your first page is where you not only hook a reader, but also a contract. Don't blow it by drowning the page in irrelevancies.

Hooking an Editor

Editors disagree about hooks and how to do them. The subtext of the hook debate, though, gets at the question I raised a few paragraphs earlier. Your opening page must, in some way, indicate to the reader why the story starts *here* rather than *elsewhere*. As an editor, perhaps one of four stories I read, I make a note—sometimes three to five pages later—suggesting that the story really started at that point, thus everything that came before it is superfluous scene-setting. Start your story in the wrong place, and most editors won't consider it for publication.

49. Describe what needs describing and nothing else. A good rule of thumb: Describe things that are different, not things that are commonplace. For example, there's no need to describe the booth in a stereotypical diner. Unless, of course, the booth was made from the back-end of a 1957 Chevrolet.

During your self-edit, watch for unconscious description proclivities. Some writers, for example, tend to obsess over certain body parts: Hair, eye color, skin tone, waist size.[14] If a reader encounters your characters and knows what color and length everyone's hair is, but nothing else, you might have a revision opportunity.

14: But enough about my training manuscripts.

Everything worth describing need not be described in one massive data dump, though. When some attribute becomes relevant, disclose it; if it's never relevant, don't disclose it. For example, it's okay to not describe the main character's hair until, in the third chapter, a friend comments about her new hairstyle. (It's also okay to never describe it at all.)

Many stories include descriptions of a character's apparel. But why? Unless a particular sartorial choice is relevant to the plot or deeply tied to the personality of a character, assume that all characters are clothed[15] and thus descriptions of clothing are only warranted when something significant is afoot. It logically follows then that a whole bunch of other common descriptors fall into the same trap. *Describe things that are different, not things that are commonplace.*

15: Unless you're writing erotica.

A certain type of genre-fiction reader (often, sci-fi, fantasy, or YA) sometimes complains about inadequate descriptions "because I can't picture in my head what the character or world looks like." That's fine. It's incumbent upon the reader to co-create the universe; over-prescription—even through precise, dense description blocks—does more harm than good, despite that occasional lazy readers may depend on it.

50. Decide when you're done. When is a story done? When you're done. Pick a point then let it go. You'll inevitably reach a point where ongoing refinement yields decreasing returns. When more effort isn't leading to noticeably better content, put a fork in it.

Next Steps 8

You've surveyed your motivation, built a personal slush pile, found a writers' tribe, and armed yourself with reference materials. Now what?

8.1 A Recapitulation

Throughout this book, we've explored a launch strategy for emerging long-form fiction writers that prioritizes the "start small" approach. Even though every year a few writers pen their first novel and sell it to national acclaim, this pathway proves exceptionally narrow. I believe it's better to build a framework for success than to hope for miracles—to walk the Path of Labor instead of the Path of Serendipity—because this framework, although it takes years to develop, will move you from the Zero Percenter to the Ten Percenter territory with a greater probability of success.

To thrive in this start-small model, you must possess a good mind for both your long- and short-term goals, as well as clear-eyed understanding of the economic misalignments among industry stakeholders. You almost surely won't make a profit by writing, but you'll make new friends and expand your own horizons by honing your literary talent. And who knows? Every year, new people break into that rarified cohort of authors who make real money from their writing. Your odds of joining their number increase when you plan your path and do the work.

I think it's generally not helpful to start your journey with a novel, because novels are hard to write. In fact, people who start from nowhere and dive into the big, beautiful passion project they've been dreaming about for years, often end up kneecapping the passion project's viability by being too hasty. Instead, fine-tune your short fiction and poetry. Work with critique groups. Be deliberate in what you study and how. Write a few "training novels," perhaps with the support of National Novel Writing Month. Only after you've spent some time practicing the art and refining your technique will you prove up to the challenge of giving that passion project the attention and the competence it deserves.

Being a *published author* isn't the same thing as being a *writer*, though. No law requires you to seek publication; in fact, an obsession for publication often diminishes the joy of creation. If you want to write, then write. Don't stress about contracts and agents. If that time ever comes, it won't be after you wrap your very first manuscript—in fact, most successful writers keep a file of a half-dozen unpublishable early training manuscripts. Because—as I've said—*novels are hard.*

Plus, focusing on publication means you also have to engage in platform building and marketing and all the ancillary parts of being in the public eye. For almost every author, those ancillary parts consume significant time and offer very little short-term payoff, although they're crucial for long-term commercial success.

Even though breaking into national-level commercial publication is wickedly difficult, it's not impossible. Just don't obsess about it. Instead, begin that long and tedious process by evaluating your personal goals and then laying a strategic foundation for achieving them. It's said that luck favors the prepared. Build your luck by being deliberate about all the building blocks of professionalism. The manifestation of that professionalism in your query package—and not raw talent alone—is what gets you past the instinctive urge of editors and agents to find the first reason to reject your submission.

Our focus in this book addressed the literary start-up sequence assuming you're willing to smart small and improve incrementally. If you engage in something like the Get Fit to Print plan—working your way through literary journals and anthologies and drafting a half-dozen practice novels—and then you find yourself in a place where you're truly ready to develop and shop your passion project . . . then what?

For starters, you'll need two things. The first is a frank assessment by a skilled book editor about the viability of your *magnum opus*. That process will prove expensive, and you may find that even more edits await, but that magisterial thumbs-up / thumbs-down lets you know whether you're on track. If you're not—well, keep at it. But if you are, and if the project is truly viable in a financial as well as a literary sense, then you're ready to seek an agent.

Despite that I'm a huge fan of small presses, a well-done debut novel endorsed by an independent editor probably should be shopped to tiny markets only after you encounter a repeated lack of interest from established agents, and only after you're convinced that the book probably lacks a national market. It's easy to fall into a trap of publishing exclusively with super-small presses. Yes, you'll enjoy easier access to publication and a shelf of published books. But you won't gain meaningful exposure. You may not care about exposure, in which case—go for whatever market will publish you. Again, a good head for your long-term goals becomes paramount. And the same logic applies to self-publishing. Although you're free to self-publish, many emerging authors find that self-publishing becomes a trap they cannot escape. So they'll have their books, but they'll rarely break through the cycle to find a willing agent on the other end of a query letter.

The second thing you'll need is a mental map for moving beyond the figurative Month 13. After all, writing those practice novels will occupy your next several years, so while you're noodling on them, you should continue your growth trajectory by becoming a master mechanic, shopping targeted material to targeted markets, building a writing business, growing your platform, and sharpening your industry acumen.

Let's briefly explore each of those ideas.

8.2 Become a Master Mechanic

One reason that we focus so heavily on writing tribes is because a high-functioning critique group reveals gaps in your skill you didn't realize were actually gaps. We're all blind to errors we don't recognize as errors, after all. But it's not enough to simply react to these external observations. You must continue to develop your literary chops.

The word *craft* sometimes assumes a snarky undertone, particularly with folks accustomed to program fiction. Yet *craft* need not be a five-letter word; instead, respect its antecedent meaning of "honed skillset" and, well, *practice the hell out of it*.

Craft-building growth follows from four interrelated practices:

1. *Read challenging material from diverse voices.* If you don't read classics and poems and genre fiction and biographies, you don't get a sense of other authors' strengths and weaknesses. When you read, look for what does and doesn't work; successful writers always both read and meta-read new material.[1] And look, at least occasionally, at stuff that crosses cultural divides—because the stylistic approach of a U.S.-based white male sci-fi writer contrasts strongly against a South African-based black female romance writer, which contrasts strongly against a low-caste Indian writer of contemporary fiction, which contrasts strongly against indigenous Canadian lesbian writers of sword-and-sorcery epics. And, yes, you really do need conversational fluence with Dead White European Males, too; any writer unfamiliar with Shakespeare and Milton and the greats of the Dread Western Canon ought to have his crayons seized. In short: *read omnivorously*.
2. *Workshop your material with other tribes on occasion*. Your tribe will help you grow. But your tribe isn't all-knowing and all-seeing. You'll find much value in taking stuff you've polished to perfection with your tribe to other writers' groups or to local author retreats. Get someone else's opinion. You'll find that different groups tend to focus on different things, as a function of each group's composition and editorial biases. Cross-comparing other groups' feedback will therefore help you take the good and make it truly great.
3. *Work with a professional contract editor*. Pro editors aren't cheap, but because you're paying them by the page, you know that you won't have any punches pulled. Start simple with something like a first-chapter critique. You'll find that a professional editor—because you're paying for the service—will bedazzle you with all sorts of observations about both the line-level quality as well as the structural quality of the work. Editors differ in their experience and skillset. Look for a grammar purist with significant experience as an independent book editor over the cheaper just-getting-started youngster. Kids these days are usually far too permissive about syntactical foibles that the grizzled old veterans eat for lunch.
4. *Write outside your comfort zone*. Even if you only aspire to write space operas, use your personal writing time to scratch a poem every now and then. Write an essay or a flash piece in a different genre. Just as weightlifters build impressive bodies by working different muscle groups with different exercises, so also do writers build impressive bodies (of work) by exercising different forms of writing.

1: As discussed in Chapter 6.

8.3 Target Your Markets

If publication remains on your radar, then develop a personal slush pile and shop it religiously. Editors and agents—despite their warm-fuzzy-inclusive bromides—are usually quite conservative in their acquisition strategies. Few have the gumption to take the financial risk of being the first to try a brand-spankin'-new writer. So build your credibility by shopping your short-form stuff with lit journals, anthologies, and contests. And start small, with niche markets. The more credits on your list, the more a somewhat lazy editor at a larger press will be inclined to give you the benefit of the doubt, given that you've already been social-proofed by her peers.

Of course, the best way to earn those first few acceptances is to be selective in your targeting strategy. Don't shotgun queries around the planet. Look for the "right" place—the annual *Writer's Market* helps—and see what kind of response you get after your first 100 submissions.[2] Unlike novels, where smaller markets sometimes prove disadvantageous, in short fiction market size is, for the most part, irrelevant. The only people who obsess over the prestige markets are the folks adjacent to academic writing programs or recent MFA grads.

2: Yes, *really* 100. Given universally low acceptance rates, rejections or silence from a mere handful of submits tells you nothing at all about the track you're on.

8.4 Build a Writing Business

It's natural for aspiring writers to pen their first novel and then, as they begin the query process, to explore whether they need a business structure to support their emerging author identity. The question is a complex one, which depends on your motivation for writing and your expectation for both income and self-made sales.[3]

3: *The Diction Dude Essential Guide to the Business of Writing* will address all of the content in this section in much greater detail. However, that volume isn't scheduled for release until 2021. If you're eager to get started before The Diction Dude weighs in, check out Helen Sedwick's *Self-Publisher's Legal Handbook* and Jane Friedman's *The Business of Being a Writer* for excellent treatments of the legal and financial aspects of professional writing. Both of these books are covered in Chapter 6.

Important

The information that follows in Section 8.4 is offered as general information only and is not intended to serve as legal, tax, or financial advice. The Diction Dude is not a licensed attorney, accountant, or insurance agent. Always consult with a licensed attorney, accountant, or insurance agent in your community who is skilled with small-business and intellectual-property matters.

Risks versus Rewards

The chief risk related to your author business boils down to one word: *complexity*. Many authors who write part-time and occasionally sell a story or two will likely find that the additional financial and legal overhead of running a parallel business structure doesn't make a ton of sense.

Starting even a bare-bones business requires the filing of paperwork with either your state or county governments, with associated fees and usually some requirement for annual-report filing. A local business registration, usually called a Certificate of Assumed Name or something similar, provides a legal pseudonym for an individual person acting in a

4: People sometimes call these assumed names DBAs, short for *doing business as*.

business capacity.[4] For example, author Sarah Jones may write under the pen name of Susan Smith. A DBA filed with the county clerk as "Susan Smith" provides a legal record attesting that legal and financial documents (including checks!) in the Susan Smith name actually refer to Sarah Jones, and that Sarah Jones is legally responsible for the Susan Smith business name. This form of county-level filing instantiates a sole proprietorship, which is a form of business organization that generates a new entity that's legally and financially coterminous with the person who created it.

Proprietorships don't offer much legal protection, but they at least establish a business name—with which, you may open a Post Office box, obtain a custom domain name, and create a website and email account.

License and Registration

Creating a business entity—registering it—isn't the same thing as obtaining a business license. Some jurisdictions require anyone engaged in business to obtain a license from the city or county government. This license allows a registered business entity to operate within the jurisdiction. Requirements for licensure and registration vary, and in some cases, separate licensure is required if you collect sales tax.

This is where the chief reward for an author business entity comes in. Even a DBA offers at least a paper-thin wall of separation between your real-life identity and your author identity. When your name gets "out there" among an ecosystem of unknown readers, you cannot control which readers may fixate on you or your family. Making it harder for people to track down the place you live proves a common-sense measure that will prove useful in the rare but not unheard-of moments when angry or emotionally compromised readers cross the line.

Levels of Complexity

For true hobbyists, either doing nothing or recording a DBA makes sense. If you sell a story or two each year to a lit journal or an anthology, there's probably no need to get crazy. Most writers, in fact, forego business structures altogether—a question you should discuss with your family attorney or CPA. For typical low-volume, low-exposure fiction writers, your potential legal risk is very small and your income is almost always low enough to wrap into standard hobbyist income-and-expense categories on your personal tax returns.

But the use cases for more complex business structures aren't exactly rare:

1. Authors who prolifically self-publish their books and then sell them in-person at various craft or writing events will likely benefit from a business banking account and a federal Employer Identification number (the business equivalent of a Social Security number). A FEIN plus a commercial bank account opens the door to a merchant card-processing account, which is handy to complete in-person sales (or sales on your website!) when cash isn't an option. To obtain a FEIN and to appropriately segregate your writing income from

your personal finances, a business entity like a limited liability company or even a subchapter-S corporation may make sense. LLCs and S-corps are rare for hobbyist authors, but full-time authors who manage their own inventory and sales may find this approach beneficial.

2. Authors who write subjects that may incur lawsuit risk—including independent investigative journalists, unauthorized biographers, and some memoirists—may benefit from insurance coverage to protect against financial ruin should you be sued for defamation or invasion of privacy. This level of risk usually also entails a business structure to further isolate the writer's personal assets from professional liability. This type of writer absolutely must work with both an attorney and an insurance broker to accurately estimate relative risk and optimal coverage levels.
3. Authors who write full-time and live on the proceeds probably need a business entity to ensure that author earnings are correctly accounted for. As a rule, you must pay yourself a reasonable salary and pay taxes on what you pay yourself. Full-time, for-income writing isn't all that common nowadays, but if that's your reality, you may run afoul of tax authorities if you don't properly account for, and allocate, your revenue between the business and your personal tax return. You certainly *can* just pay personal taxes on all your royalties, but you may find it more advantageous from a tax perspective to channel revenue and expenses through a business structure. Talk to your CPA for guidance.

What Do You Need?

Although the specific form and degree of business structure depends on your conversations with your attorney and your accountant, prepare for that discussion by considering the following use cases:

Privacy protection Authors who publish material should, as a matter of privacy protection, enjoy a wall of separation between their personal life and their author identity. Whether this wall comes from merely writing under pseudonym, or filing a DBA, or establishing a more formal business entity like a proprietorship or an LLC or an S-Corp, is a function of both your goals and your expected visibility and revenue potential.

Marketing A specific brand around an author persona protects your writing brand and facilitates future sales and networking. Although you don't need a business structure to establish this brand, filing a business entity in the name of the author persona at least protects against encroachment within the scope of your state or county.[5]

5: Business licensing authorities won't allow substantially the same business names; it's first-come, first-served, generally.

Personal retail sales If you regularly sell your own books, as many self-published authors do, then at a certain point, a business structure that supports a commercial banking account may make sense—at the least, to process credit cards and segregate any sales tax you may owe to your state or local government.[6]

6: Authors must assess applicable sales tax when they sell their own books, even though most don't.

Insurance Although it's rare, some authors may benefit from certain forms of liability coverage.

Salary reporting A full-time writer who lives off his writing-related income must properly account for revenue, expenses, tax liability, and the salary he or she must pay to himself. In most cases, a business entity facilitates that work while offering the most favorable tax implications, although there are quite a few substantially different strategies that may work for author compensation.

The Most Important Rule?

Don't fret. Business entities—if they make sense for you at all—don't need to be established as soon as you decide to write. If your writing as a non-business hobbyist blooms, re-consider your options. Given that many hobbyist authors never create a business entity, it's not something to stress over before you've finished a manuscript.

Consider your goals and your most likely financial trajectory as a writer then discuss options with your attorney and accountant.

8.5 Grow Your Platform

If you skip a formal business structure, you nevertheless probably do need something as basic as a website and an email domain, and probably social-media accounts in the name of your author identity. It's often helpful for people to write under some sort of pseudonym, if only to protect your real-life identity from readers and fans. So a domain and website—and probably social accounts on Facebook, Twitter, and Goodreads—make sense. From there, stuff like give-away materials (e.g., bookmarks) help connect to readers.

Some authors create business cards. You're welcome to do so, but be careful about putting your real contact information on them. It does you no good to adopt an author persona but then put your real phone number or email address on the card.

Two important points about platform:

First, *build a mailing list*. That's what agents and editors are most keen to see; in fact, some publishers require that you send a list of a minimum number of viable names and email addresses to facilitate early sales. So solicit every opportunity to add viable names to your author mail list—sign-ups at events and on your website work well for this purpose—and encourage followers on social media. For an editor, a large mailing list translates to some proportion of likely purchasers of a book in the first calendar quarter after it's released. That sales contribution can make-or-break a borderline estimated profit-and-loss statement. P&Ls, for many publishers, determine whether a proposed book project will prove financially viable. The bigger your list, the more favorable that P&L becomes.

Second, *use your blog to introduce yourself to your audience.* Blog frequently then amplify your posts through your social-media accounts. Do not rely on social media alone—everything should link back to your blog. Use it to share reflections about writing or early drafts of work. In general, if you publish content on your blog, you can't sell it to a commercial market, given that blog publishing is still publishing. However, flash fiction or poems you don't intend to shop may make excellent candidates for posts, as do reflections about your growth as a writer and even stuff like character sketches.

In light of the Get Fit to Print program, and knowing that hobbyist authors flower over a period of years, it probably makes sense early on to do a few things, even before you've written anything for publication:

- Choose an author name and potentially a tagline
- Purchase a domain name using your author name
- Establish an email account using your domain name
- Establish author-focused social-media accounts that aren't tied to your personal social accounts
- Start a blog and publish something two to four times per month at first, sharing those posts to your social accounts
- Start a mailing list that supports signups on your website

More tech-savvy or marketing-advanced emerging authors may even consider a podcast, or an author logo and stationery, or an author-focused YouTube channel. The only caveat is that the more you invest in marketing without a product to sell, the less interest you'll retain among your followers.

8.6 Boost Your Acumen

Pay attention to industry trends. Keep an eye on awards and sales trajectories and best-seller lists. Watch things like mergers and acquisitions among publishers and distributors.

Publishing isn't a hard industry to comprehend, but it's a hard industry to navigate if you haven't figured out the basics. Part of the challenge lies in appreciating the uncertainty that's part of the core industry dynamic. From a business perspective, agents and presses come and go at a dizzying rate. From an economic perspective, the money going into different genres and formats varies from year to year. But one thing is certain: Beyond an 18-month horizon, no publishing executive anywhere knows what the Next Big Thing will be.

Blogs about the industry are plentiful. Most are crap, but if you start with places like *Writers Digest* and *Poets & Writers*, you'll be sufficiently clued in to big-picture dynamics.

Be cautious, however, about by-author-for-author sites and services. Quite often, the information presented there is shallow and one-sided. When possible, go to the source directly (e.g., agent blogs) or follow journalism about the industry, rather than author self-help forums and the like.[7]

7: Some sites are quite good; most are mediocre, a small amount are toxic.

8.7 Parting Encouragement

The Internet and even bookstore shelves offer writing advice that ranges from insipid to inspired. Many of these resources tell you that you can do it.

And you know what?

You *can* do it. You can knock it outta the park. But there's a catch. You must saddle up to the plate with a deep and unvarnished understanding of your unique strengths and weaknesses as a contender. Not everyone can or should swing for the fences from their first at-bat; sometimes, you've got to bunt or aim for the single or the double while you perfect your line drive. Self-awareness about your relative level of skill and connectedness, as well as a sense of what the industry is and isn't looking for, helps you pick the right model for publication—or choose to delay or skip the rejection-slip grind altogether.

Self-awareness also helps you understand the optimal path for starting where you are then growing into the place you aspire to be.

I get upset sometimes with writing advice that distils to "write every day and eventually success will find you." Over the years I've met very many writers who followed that advice. And success never found them. And why should it? Success never comes without effort; mere repetition at the keyboard isn't enough. Too many experts substitute warm-fuzzy slogans for clear-headed guidance.

Writing isn't easy, even for people with a natural aptitude for language. And writing *for commercial publication?* That's even harder—because not only do you have to write flawless prose or verse that meets a specific and hard-to-predict market need, but you must also be effective at marketing and networking and all sorts of other things that separate national book tours from self-signups for local author meetups.

The joy of writing is *writing*, not publication, however. In Chapter 3's opening essay, I mentioned my first painful experience with National Novel Writing Month. I've participated in NaNoWriMo for nearly a decade now. Why? Because I thrive on 30 frenetic days of being surrounded by people who love new ideas and story prompts and plot bunnies and all the things that make writing *fun*.

Fun is important. Treasure it. Not many people experience the joy of creating something as complex and rich and beautiful as a story.

No matter whether your work is destined for *The New York Times* bestseller list or just a dusty part of your own hard drive, take joy in the crafting and in the journey, for writing isn't about a book on the shelf but rather about the thrill of creating beautiful stories, one sentence at a time.

You really can do it. Just be smart about it. Avoid magical thinking and don't take shortcuts. The Diction Dude believes in you.

Appendix

Glossary A

The following commonly used terms in the industry have appeared in this book. The list appears alphabetically.

adult trade Books channel into several markets with different standards, price points, and distribution systems. Most novels intended for a broad reading audience fall into the market called *adult trade*.

advance review copy A mostly final pre-production version of a book released early to select audiences to facilitate either final proofreading or pre-release reviews. ARCs are either hard (print) or soft (ebook or PDF).

agents An agent works on behalf of an author to place a manuscript with a major publisher. Agents work on a commission paid directly from author advances and royalties.

appropriation narratives Stories with a deep hook into the culture or historical experience of a specific human population, but told by a person who lacks membership in that population. This practice is increasingly disfavored, particularly when the population in question is historically disadvantaged but the writer is not.

author as customer A business approach by writers that assumes that they're the customers of agents and publishers and therefore are entitled to be treated as such.

author as supplier A business approach by writers that assumes they're suppliers of content (manuscripts) to agents and publishers and therefore comport themselves to a specific, yet important, role in the literary supply chain.

cancel culture A tendency by some activists of the Left to deny economic opportunity and social esteem to people who don't share their sociopolitical biases. Cancel culture is significant in some publishing genres, and it often includes public campaigns of harassment and intimidation—for both the "canceled" person as well as the institutions affiliated with that person.

colorspace A method for identifying color. The two most common colorspaces in publishing are CMYK (cyan, magenta, yellow, key/black) and RGB (red, green, blue). CMYK is optimized for four-process printing on paper while RGB is optimized for on-screen displays. The colorspaces use different codes and values to represent specific colors, which aren't perfectly interchangeable.

commercially viable author An author whose book is expected to perform reasonably well in the open market, and who can support that book with both a platform and a baseline degree of professionalism, is considered viable for a commercial book contract.

contracts A contract is any legal agreement, but in publishing, it's often shorthand for contracts governing long-form books like novels.

distribution catalogs A distributor releases one or more catalogs that segment books by intended market—children's, adult trade, textbooks, etc. Retail buyers subscribe to different catalogs.

distribution networks The industry supports several different book distributors, which act as wholesale middlemen between publishers and retailers. Any retail buyer participates with one or more distributors. Most retailers order from the Ingram catalog, at a minimum, but so many books are in Ingram that it's hard for any given title to rise to buyers' attention—which is why major presses hire sales agents to persuade buyers to pick their preferred titles. Several smaller distribution networks focus on specific genres. The proliferation of distributors means that very small, general-interest presses are effectively priced out of participation in the full distribution ecosystem.

fusion A blending of genres. Some blended genres are already recognized as new genres in their own right (e.g., supernatural romance) while more exotic pairings defy easy categorization (e.g., bisexual aliens in ancient Rome). Non-standard genres, because they're difficult to classify in metadata and hard to place on a single, consistent bookshelf, often face obstacles to commercial publication.

gatekeepers of the industry Any institution—an agent or an editor with a small press—that receives cold pitches from the general public serves as the first-line gatekeepers. Then, the acquisitions editors at large presses serve as second-line gatekeepers of agented manuscripts.

gatekeeping Gatekeeping in general is the process of assessing literary merit and financial viability before considering a given book for publication. The term often relates specifically to the practice of editors and agents making yes-or-no judgments about queries pending in the slush pile.

hybrid publishing An innovation in the industry, hybrid publishers combine the gatekeeping (q.v.) of conventional publishing companies with financial engagement by the author to mitigate the cost of publishing an editorially worthwhile but financially weak title. A well-run hybrid may be an ideal option for good works with small market potential, although some shady subsidy presses (q.v.) sometimes co-opt the term for nefarious purposes.

Ingram A major distributor and print-on-demand service. Most bookstores use at least the Ingram catalog. Ingram maintains a self-publish wing called IngramSpark that supports both self-published authors and micro-press editors.

Jessica Fletcher syndrome The tendency of some emerging writers to act as if full-time writing ought to be easy, highly compensated, and full of adulation for the author.

license agreements A legal document that allows the licensee (usually a publisher) to reprint or otherwise publish the creative work of the licensor. In everyday publishing parlance, a license agreement often refers to short-form works like poems and short stories, while the term *contracts* (q.v.) refers to long-form works like novels—despite that the agreements are contracts and novel contracts are essentially license agreements.

Man Booker prize A prestigious literary award presented for the best original novel written in English and published in the United Kingdom. As of June 2019, it's been renamed to the Booker Prize for Fiction.

market Any institution—agents, agencies, publishers—that works with authors to publish works of literary and financial merit.

MFA Writers and poets who pursue a Master of Fine Arts program generally focus on reading and craft development. MFA-prepared creators tend to engage in literary culture. An MFA is unlikely to be aligned with a doctoral program in English, which in some literary and academic circles is a contributor to tension between MFAs and PhDs.

micro-presses The smallest classification of small presses. They are traditional presses, but they usually publish fewer than a dozen titles per year. They lack meaningful sales reach, but they often prove willing to take a risk on good, but hard-to-market, content.

mid-list author A type of genre-fiction author who reliably turned out books that did well enough. They rarely became household names but they usually broke even or better for their publishers.

National Novel Writing Month An orgy of noveling held every November. Participants in this free, global program must write 50,000 words (which may or may not be a complete book!) in 30 days to "win." Many regions of NaNoWriMo feature active communities and in-person writing events, both in November and throughout the year.

pantsing Writing by the seat of one's pants—informally, a pantser is a person who writes stories without meaningful planning.

Path of Labor Recognizing that writing for commercial markets is hard and requires a careful plan and significant preparation.

Path of Serendipity Hoping that luck will strike and you'll somehow, as if by magic, become a Very Important Author.

platform The term of art for an author's total marketing infrastructure. Usually, platform is measured in terms of the size of a qualified email list or the typical reach of the author's social-media posts. Platform factors into a provisional profit-and-loss statement (q.v.) insofar as a larger platform translates to a greater number of estimated sales of a book in the first calendar quarter after it's released.

profit and loss statements A provisional P&L represents a publisher's best estimate about the expected financial performance of a given book. These documents account for the costs of production and the expected sale relative to competitive titles. Concerns about a book's market viability often reflect an unfavorable P&L.

program fiction A mode of writing—both in substance and in style—that's common to graduate-level writing programs. Much current literary fiction is a form of program fiction.

proposal A highly structured document that pitches a work of non-fiction to an agent or an editor. Non-fiction books rarely get written before they're proposed. Fiction books are pitched through a *query* (q.v.).

published author Writers who obtain publication (either through a commercial publisher, or through self-publishing services) such that other people can buy or read the writers' work product, is considered a published author. Authors are a subset of writers.

purple prose Writing that's garishly ornate. Overblown. Full of itself.

query A package of information—usually a cover letter and manuscript, or a cover letter with a synopsis and sample—intended to induce an agent or a small-press editor to publish a work of fiction. Non-fiction works are pitched through a *proposal* (q.v.).

self publishing The act of producing, distributing, and selling a book by an author directly, without licensing those functions to others.

slush pile A collection of manuscripts. For authors, a personal slush pile includes a bunch of work that's ready to be shopped to a market (q.v.) at a moment's notice. For agents and small-press editors, the slush pile is the collection of unsolicited manuscripts authors have submitted for review.

subsidy press Subsidy presses—usually called, derogatorily, *vanity presses*—are pay-to-publish outfits that pass along the full cost (and then some) to the author for the privilege of developing a book. Although some subsidy presses are legitimate, many of them are predatory or outright scams. The number of valid use cases for a subsidy press is small.

Ten Percenter An experienced, skilled, and networked author who still earns rejections, but much less often than her less-well-positioned peers.

traditional publishers Publishing companies are considered *traditional* if they exercise subjective editorial gatekeeping over inbound manuscripts and assume the full financial risk of a book's potential poor performance.

training manuscript Training manuscripts hone the author's craft and support experimentation in new techniques. They're not intended for publication. For many writers, the first half-dozen novels they write are training manuscripts.

typeface A typeface is a named family of fonts that share the same characteristics. For example, the Garamond typeface includes the Garamond Italic and the Garamond Bold fonts.

via negativa The philosophical method of subtraction. It's an approach to concept clarification that emphasizes things to not-do or to avoid.

writer Writers are people who write poetry, fiction, technical non-fiction, and creative non-fiction, regardless of whether other people read it. Some writers become published authors (q.v.).

zero draft A chuck-the-words-on-the-page approach to drafting that favors speed and word count over polish. Generally, a complete zero draft—after it's had its first stem-to-stern revision by the author—becomes a first draft.

Zero Percenter People whose lack of above-average skill or a large network mean they'll experience almost no acceptances with traditional publishers.

Acknowledgements | B

I'm grateful to my colleagues Lisa and Brittany, each of whom reviewed in detail several early chapters of this book's antecedent massive and overly complicated first iteration—i.e., when *The Diction Dude Essential Guides Series* was one sprawling mess of a book weighing in at a targeted 250,000 words. In addition, several of our interns at Caffeinated Press reviewed sections of that first iteration; Mitchell and Rose, in particular, offered substantial helpful feedback. My friend Jason very kindly conducted a high-level proofread of the final PDF and caught several embarrassing syntactical foibles and typesetting inconsistencies. Any errors that remain accrue solely to the author.

I must credit the love and support and the on-point challenges I've enjoyed from "my tribes"—the (former) Caffeinated Press family, WriteOn!, the Grand River Writing Tribe, the OCGR Wrimos, and the excellent annual retreats sponsored by the MiFiWriters.

As I've said: Writing is a solo act, but being a *professional writer* takes a tribe. I'm incredibly blessed by the richness of mine. Build your own tribe! Even if you only end up half as lucky as I, you'll still be twice as prepared as the next person in the slush pile. And that ain't no small thing.

About the Author C

Jason Gillikin founded Lakeshore Literary—a small traditional and hybrid Midwestern publisher and specialty book distributor—and Diction Dude, an author-consulting and freelance writing-and-editing agency. He's a co-founder and former CEO of Caffeinated Press, which operated between 2014 and 2019, in which capacity he served as publisher of *The 3288 Review*, Caffeinated Press's journal of arts and letters.

Gillikin got his start as a newspaper columnist in the twilight of the second millennium, working up the ranks until he earned appointment as editor-in-chief of *The Western Herald*, a small daily community broadsheet. He's freelanced as a writer and editor for several national media corporations, where his content has earned more than 4 million distinct impressions on the Web and he coached several hundred general-assignment writers. Simultaneously, he's the facilitator of the Grand River Writing Tribe, a small writers' collective in the heart of West Michigan.

His published work includes a personal essay in *Christ's Body, Christ's Wounds* (Cascade Books, 2018), a speculative-fiction novelette in *Division by Zero: Double Take* (MiFiWriters, 2018), a peer-reviewed entry into the *Encyclopedia of Survey Research Methods* (SAGE Publications, 2008) and a technical essay in *America Now* (Bedford/St. Martins, 2003). This work is in addition to his byline and non-byline work as an online service journalist and his published columns, editorials, and news stories from the *Herald*.

He earned a degree in applied ethics and quantitative political science from Western Michigan University. In his free time, he is an avid hiker, scuba diver, and cat butler.

For more information, visit dictiondude.com.

Bibliography

The references within this book are cited below, in the order in which they appeared.

[1] Michael Bourne. 'A Day in the Life of a Book Editor: Caroline Bleeke of Flatiron Books'. In: *Poets & Writers* 46.5 (2018) (cited on page 5).

[2] Becky Tuch. *More Work, No Pay: Why I Detest 'Literary Citizenship'*. Salon.com. Apr. 2014. URL: https://www.salon.com/2014/04/23/more_work_no_pay_why_i_detest_literary_citizenship/ (cited on page 5).

[3] The Authors Guild. *Authors Guild Survey Shows Drastic 42 Percent Decline in Authors Earnings in Last Decade*. Jan. 2019. URL: https://www.authorsguild.org/industry-advocacy/authors-guild-survey-shows-drastic-42-percent-decline-in-authors-earnings-in-last-decade/ (cited on pages 6, 21, 30, 54).

[4] Elif Batuman. 'Get a Real Degree'. In: *London Review of Books* 32.18 (2010) (cited on page 7).

[5] Federico Pistono. *Traditional vs Self-Publishing, How Much Money Can You Really Make?* Medium.com. Jan. 2017. URL: https://medium.com/@FedericoPistono/traditional-vs-self-publishing-how-much-money-can-you-really-make-c5732afeabaf (cited on page 8).

[6] WikiHow. *How to Become a Published Writer*. May 2019. URL: https://www.wikihow.com/Become-a-Published-Writer (cited on page 9).

[7] Austin Hendrix and Roman Yampolskiy. 'Automated IQ Estimation from Writing Samples.' In: *MAICS*. 2017, pp. 3–7 (cited on page 10).

[8] Annabelle GY Lim. *The Big Five Personality Traits*. SimplyPsychology. June 2020. URL: https://www.simplypsychology.org/big-five-personality.html (cited on page 10).

[9] US Census Bureau. *Number of Firms, Number of Establishments, Employment, Annual Payroll, and Preliminary Reciepts by Enterprise Employment Size for the United States, All Industries: 2017*. Tech. rep. U.S. Census Bureau, Mar. 2020 (cited on page 20).

[10] Steven Piersanti. *The 10 Awful Truths About Book Publishing*. Berrett-Koehler Publishers. Sept. 2016. URL: https://www.bkconnection.com/the-10-awful-truths-about-book-publishing (cited on page 21).

[11] Alison Flood. 'Authors' incomes collapse to 'abject' levels'. In: *The Guardian* (July 2014) (cited on page 21).

[12] Steve Laube. *What Are Average Book Sales?* The Steve Laube Agency. June 2019. URL: https://stevelaube.com/what-are-average-book-sales/ (cited on page 21).

[13] Kiera O'Brien and Sarah Shaffi. *Tyler is top-selling Man Booker longlisted title*. The Bookseller. Sept. 2015. URL: https://www.thebookseller.com/news/anne-tyler-top-selling-man-booker-longlisted-title-312012 (cited on page 21).

[14] Laura Jimenez. *Where Is the Diversity in Publishing? The 2019 Diversity Baseline Survey Results*. Lee and Low Books. Jan. 2020. URL: https://blog.leeandlow.com/2020/01/28/2019diversitybaselinesurvey/ (cited on page 21).

[15] Julie Bosman. 'Bookstores Stroke Trump Resistance with Action, Not Just Words'. In: *The New York Times* (Feb. 2017) (cited on page 21).

[16] Katy Waldman. 'In Y.A., Where Is the Line Between Criticism and Cancel Culture?' In: *The New Yorker* (Mar. 2019) (cited on page 22).

[17] Jane Friedman. *9 Statistics Writers Should Know About Amazon*. JaneFriedman.com. Feb. 2017. URL: https://www.janefriedman.com/9-statistics-writers-know-amazon/ (cited on page 23).

[18] Chuck Wendig. *Setting Free The Sacred Cows Of Writing Advice*. Terribleminds. June 2018. URL: http://terribleminds.com/ramble/2018/06/12/setting-free-the-sacred-cows-of-writing-advice/ (cited on page 89).

[19] Richard Nordquist. *Purple Prose*. English. ThoughtCo.com. Mar. 2019. URL: https://www.thoughtco.com/purple-prose-1691705 (cited on page 91).

[20] Michael Emmert. *An Introduction to Filtering*. Scribophile. URL: https://www.scribophile.com/academy/an-introduction-to-filtering (cited on page 105).

Alphabetical Index

CPSIA information can be obtained
at www.ICGtesting.com
Printed in the USA
BVHW012024201022
649917BV00005B/14

9 780986 380662